MILE HIGH CLUB

First class All the Way With the Rich and Famous

by Diana Benson

DOVE
B O O K S

IN MEMORY OF

Simon
Joseph
Jeffrey
John
Steve

ISBN 0-7871-1181-3

Printed in the United States of America

DOVE BOOKS
8955 Beverly Boulevard
Los Angeles, CA 90048
(310) 786-1600

Distributed by Penguin USA

Text design by Carolyn Wendt
Cover design by Rick Penn-Kraus

First Printing: June 1997

10 9 8 7 6 5 4 3 2 1

Acknowledgments

The celebrity stories in this book are all true. Every word. They were contributed by flight attendants whom I would have loved to thank individually, but who prefer to remain anonymous. The reason will become obvious as you read the book.

I can, however, express my sincere gratitude to my coworker Pattee, and other coworkers as well, for their time, effort, stories, and support. I thank Honey for her honesty in sharing her personal experiences. Thanks also to my dear friend and son, Eric, for his endless and untiring efforts to keep my computer working, and for his love and loyalty through it all.

To the passengers, personalities, celebrities, and athletes who provided the material, this is really your story.

At Dove Books: Michael, Doug, Lee, Beth, and Michelle.

To Ricky, for his talent, humor, and sexy E-mail.

To my cheerleaders, Shirlene and, on the homefront, Michael, Christina, Lisa, and especially the "flower child" in my life, dear Heather.

This book is for:

All the starry-eyed young women who dream of becoming flight attendants. Pay attention and you will learn what not *to do and* why.

The Suzy Homemakers who wonder what it would be like to be a flight attendant. Stop wondering and do it.

The eager pilots who are unsure if they are really wanted in the sky. Go for it. *We need you.*

The former MGM flight attendants. I hope you will feel vindicated. I also hope that you will laugh at yourselves and, through this book, look back fondly at our special time together in the air.

Our former passengers. I hope you have a sense of humor. (For those of you who don't, I'm sorry. Get over it.)

And, finally, this book is for all those wonderful caregivers in the sky. May all your flights be good ones, and remember to dance in the aisles.

CONTENTS

PROLOGUE

*I*ncoming traffic. As a veteran flight attendant, I know what those words mean. You're probably thinking I'm talking about some holding pattern caused by planes stacked up at JFK or O'Hare. Not this time. I'm talking about the incoming traffic of film, sports, and music celebrities about to descend on a crew of hard-working flight attendants.

It's time for what I call search and destroy, a procedure intended to gain some respect for those who deserve respect and show that many of those stars the whole world admires aren't so admirable. Of course, many of the celebrity passengers I flew with were wonderful. Some kept the whole plane laughing and others were just plain goofy. I'll happily tell about those encounters as well. Those warm and considerate celebrity passengers, as well as a great crew, made some very special memories.

Some other passengers may feel embarrassed by what

is revealed in these pages. I understand humiliation. Remember, I said I was a flight attendant—most recently for the all-first-class airline, MGM Grand Air.

In its five years of operation as a scheduled carrier, MGM Grand flew thousands of celebrities—actors, musicians, jocks, politicians, executives—each hornier than the last and only too eager to join the Mile High Club, that exclusive organization reserved for all those who could lay claim to having had sex at 12,000 feet or above. The more adventurous did it in the rear lavatory; the more reserved in their own on-board stateroom. Stateroom? You betcha! After all, this was a unique airline created for the rich and famous. The *very* rich and the *very* famous.

There were actors—Billy Baldwin, Warren Beatty, Robert DeNiro, Harrison Ford, Richard Gere, Jason Patric, Sean Penn, and O.J. Simpson (the biggest actor of all). There were actresses—Loni Anderson, Candice Bergen, Cher, Joan Collins, Bette Davis, Farrah Fawcett, Jodie Foster, Zsa Zsa Gabor, Whitney Houston, and Madonna. Entire basketball teams—among them the L.A. Lakers and Chicago Bulls. Rock groups—Guns N' Roses, U2, the Rolling Stones, the Who. And executives—network heads, studio heads, recording heads, and politicians getting head.

The airline accommodated its celebrity clientele in every way. MGM Grand redesigned the interior of its fleet of Boeing 727s as a club owner's wet dream, complete with burgundy velvet barrel seats, crystal ceiling chandeliers, and a fully equipped stand-up bar with a leather settee. And then there were the staterooms— four of them, each with burgundy curtains (for privacy) and blue velvet seating that transformed into a double bed (for screwing). Two monitors on each side of the staterooms played different movies. All the better to keep the stars from getting bored, just in case the sex was lacking in imagination.

The aforementioned aft lavatory beyond the staterooms featured a leather couch that hid the toilet. First-time passengers would walk into the lav and stop dead. I'd always give them a minute to snap out of their shock before I'd wander by and say, "Lift the leather seat first. I'm not cleaning up after you." The vanity top was marble (of course); the fixtures were brass (of course); and all the walls were mirrored (of course).

The whole thing was supposed to reek of sophistication and class. To me, it shouted Las Vegas lounge with a smattering of bordello. Fortunately, we didn't give most of our passengers much time to concentrate on their surroundings as we hopped into action soon after climbing past 10,000 feet. I'd join my fellow flight attendants to pull out the crystal stemware, cover the bar in linen, set up the sterling ice buckets stocked with fine wine and champagne, place a fresh red rose on each table set up in front of each barrel seat, and wait for the applause that we never heard.

Our act was a choreographed two-step that not

only demonstrated our teamwork but also gave the male passenger sitting on the bar settee a close-up view of our asses and legs. They would end up in his face nonstop (at no extra charge). When we were finished, the cabin was a sight to behold—all glitter and sparkle—and this even before the captain had turned off the seat-belt sign.

It was in this setting, day after day, that the rich would misbehave, the famous would attempt to become infamous, and the poor-but-privileged would get a glimpse of a world that was sometimes almost too bizarre to believe. Waiting for incoming traffic, I prepared myself for the pinching, grabbing, and groping that this planeload of passengers was about to employ.

As they approached, I did what I had learned to do after years of flying on MGM Grand Air. I clamped my legs shut and began to negotiate. "Don't mess with me and I won't mess with you," my mouth muttered. And believe me, I knew how to get back at those who deserved it. Oh, yes, I forgot to tell you. My nickname on the airline was Dirty Diana. I have a mouth that says what it thinks quicker than my brain thinks what to say. And it got me in trouble, then as now.

1 DIRTY DIANA

I'm a first-generation Italian and proud of it. More Anna Maria Alberghetti than Mama Leone, I knew from an early age that I wasn't about to spend my life over a pot of simmering pasta sauce. I kept *that* piece of news to myself, however, because in those days, the only way a good Italian girl ever got to leave home was to go directly to her husband's.

I had never thought about flying, but I knew I had to rebel against the old rules and break with the expected roles for an Italian girl graduating from high school. It wasn't simply a matter of getting a job. You see, in upstate New York in the 1960s, the only acceptable occupations for a teenage girl to look forward to—at least by Italian standards—were to become a teacher or a nurse. Neither appealed to me. If I wasn't ready to be surrounded by my own kids, I certainly didn't want to be surrounded by someone else's. And as for becoming a nurse, I didn't see myself as a quiet, soothing woman in white.

The concept of marriage left me cold as well, particularly marriage to a pre-approved Italian stud who would make certain my entire existence started and ended on Sunday with making the traditional all-day meal. I had grown up watching girls turn into women and then disappear into that kind of life—one that functioned around custom and varied only with birth, illness, and death.

Run like hell was my plan, and run I did—right into the waiting wings of American Airlines. The year was 1966, and being a stewardess—yes, that's what they called us back then—was looked upon as a prestigious and glamorous position. Sure it was sexist. Hell, we couldn't even put on a little weight without being told to take it off—and quickly. If you took too long to remove the flab, you were given diet pills without a second thought. If even that didn't work, you were off the payroll until the weight disappeared, or you did.

Sexual and age discrimination were words but not yet a whole sentence. There were other important issues for a single working woman to fight for in the 1960s—things like putting food on the table and paying the rent. Those seemingly simple tasks proved harder than I could ever have imagined. It wasn't that I wasn't getting paid. I just wasn't getting paid very much.

At the end of a month's training, American Airlines gave each of us a small check and sent us to our hub city. In my case, it was Manhattan—the Big Apple with big living expenses. I had planned to share an apartment with another new stewardess, but she became ill just before graduation and couldn't join me for weeks. For the first time in my life, I was alone.

I arrived in New York in late summer 1966 without a clue as to my next step. I walked the streets near the airport looking for a FOR RENT sign and eventually found a two-bedroom apartment. What I needed to find next were some roommates. Landlords, I later learned, upped the rent when they saw flight attendants approach. We were looked upon as high-risk tenants. The perception was that we would bail on our bills. Leave in the dead of night. So, deposits and rents were tripled.

With the need for a roommate becoming more obvious by the moment, I headed out to the airport to greet the newly arriving graduates. It seemed logical enough, since we were all in the same situation. What I hadn't counted on was competition in the person of a pimp who approached me and other desperate-looking new stewardesses with promises of free rent and expensive clothes.

I didn't think it wise to change career directions quite so soon, and after finally realizing exactly what it was I was being offered, I let out a grand old scream—one loud enough to send that pimp packing. Had I actually known how little I would make as a stewardess and how similar to prostitution some of the things I would be asked to do in the air were, I might not have been so hasty. As it was, my lot was cast with the clouds at 32,000 feet.

I eventually found a roommate, and she turned into a lifelong friend. Her name was Dee Dee (not her real name . . . well, sorta), and she was as Southern as pecan pie. We were such an odd couple. Me, the Italian Yankee Catholic; she, the Southern Baptist. We became fast friends after she unexpectedly arrived home early from a flight and walked smack into me entertaining a date.

Actually, it was one of those rare occasions when all three of my roommates were out on a flight. When I heard someone at the door, I panicked and shoved my naked stud into the hall closet. Of course, it was the first place Dee Dee headed when she entered the apartment.

I watched silently as she opened the closet door, placed her coat inside, and then closed the door again. Without missing a beat, she calmly said in her lovely Southern drawl: "Sootie"—she called me Sootie, which was a shorthand for my maiden name—"there's a very handsome naked man in our closet." After that, our relationship couldn't help but solidify.

During the year that followed, I turned this gentle, conservative belle into a crazy lady, armed and ready to accompany me on any adventure. We decided we would buddy bid (fly together), and we worked great as a team, on and off duty.

She loved the snow but couldn't ever get the hang of boots. She preferred to let me lead the way and followed meekly in my footprints. She even started to learn Italian, and I helped her impress any Italian passengers. She'd run back to the galley and ask me to teach her an Italian phrase. I would, of course, teach her something vulgar, and then tell her it meant something entirely different. Poor thing would skip down the aisle, eager to repeat the line to her passenger. Each time, she would come back dejected, certain that she had made some silly mistake because the phrase hadn't gotten the desired response.

Nothing seemed to be beyond our reach. One time we stole an airport fire truck, with me behind the wheel. We were quite the sight, skirts hiked up, long white scarves billowing, doing our impression of the Red Baron.

That episode paled by comparison to the time we drove a VW Bug through the automatic doors at LaGuardia, right past the ticket counter, and grabbed a standing life-size poster of one Pattee Paulson. We hated Pattee. She was American's model stewardess— blond, blue-eyed, gorgeous, and perfect. Well, Dee Dee drove the getaway car while I held Pattee out the window. To this day, I believe the only reason we weren't fired on the spot was that all the ticket agents shared our opinion of Little Miss Perfect.

Yes, Dee Dee and I were inseparable in those days. Lucky for her, she somehow missed joining me on my inaugural flight. As usual, I was running slightly behind, if only because I wanted everything to look perfect—my hair, my nails, even my teeth needed to shine with extra sparkle. I remember checking in late for my first flight. In fact, I had been running so hard,

I could barely speak when I finally found Crew Scheduling to check in. Terror was probably written all over my face. It didn't help that airline personnel could smell the fear of a new crew member a mile away.

I was so excited that first day, walking on board an American 727, wearing my new uniform complete with white gloves and Jackie pillbox hat. I stood there, a smile fixed to my lips, my eyes shining in anticipation, as I greeted arriving passengers.

Greeting, serving the meal, saying good-bye—ah, yes, saying good-bye. Despite what I would undergo later with the passengers on MGM, my most embarrassing moment in the air was on my first flight (it could have been my last). We had just completed that first flight and my final duty was to lower the aft stairs to deplane the passengers from coach. (In those days, the jetway had yet to be invented.)

There I was, having successfully withstood the rigors of flight number one. I thought I was the hottest thing on the plane as I bid my passengers farewell. "Good-bye. Have a nice day. Come back." With my Miss America smile and gloved handshake, I knew these good folks would all go home remembering me and send wonderful, glowing letters to the president of American.

Yet, the entire time I was saying good-bye, I kept hearing this sound . . . an annoying ringing in my ears. I discovered that it was actually the on-board intercom after a fellow stew pulled me aside and said that the captain wanted to speak to me. For some reason, I had taken my uniform to heart a bit (actually a lot) too seriously and grabbed the flight phone. "Can I get back to you? I'm busy deplaning the passengers."

"I'm aware of what the hell you're doing. I just want to know *why* the fuck you're doing it!" the pissed-off captain shot back over the phone. "We're not at the fucking terminal yet. We just stopped for a moment. Who the hell said to drop the stairs?" He screamed loud enough for the entire plane to hear.

I noticed the giggling stews in front of me and dropped the phone. One of the senior stewardesses just gestured to the stairs and crossed her arms across her chest. As I got to the bottom step, I couldn't believe my eyes. Moving, confused bodies in motion. My passengers looked like lost children searching for their mother.

One man screamed, "What the hell is this? Can't we get closer to the airport?"

"Sir, you did fly coach," was the best comeback I could offer as I hustled them back on the plane.

Once I raised the aft stairs, I ran into the lav and didn't come out until the cleaners kicked me out. I learned to ask a lot of questions and move a little slower that day. In its own way, it prepared me for the assortment of indignities to come, many at the hands of the world's most famous stars.

It was while I was flying with American that I had my first celebrity encounter. The very sexy Harry Belafonte was on one of my inaugural flights. He cornered me in the galley and asked if I'd like to attend his concert and spend the evening with him. I informed him that this was just one leg of the flight scheduled for me that day.

"So get off and stay anyway," he told me.

I was twenty years old, obviously naive, and this stranger wanted me to bail on a new job just to run off with him for one night. I thought he was crazy. Maybe I was. Certainly the other stews thought so. Little did I know that such offers, and my rejection of them, would become commonplace.

My parents persuaded me to move back to the comforts of home and family and take a break from flying, but eventually, lured by the sway of palm trees and the blissful lack of snow, I gave up Sunday pasta dinners for tofu, alfalfa sprouts, fresh fruit, and the nuts of California.

In Los Angeles every Friday evening after work, my roommate and I would meet in a bar to eat steak sandwiches and shoot pool. What I lacked in talent with a cue and eight ball, I more than made up for with my micro-miniskirt. It attracted the attention of a gorgeous hunk one night, a George Hamilton look-alike who undressed me with a quick strip of his eyes and then proceeded to pass out.

We had what you could call a whirlwind courtship—four months of romance ending in a trip to New York in mid-1969. I thought I was in love, I knew I was in lust, and I was only too happy to tell everyone I found, including my parents.

The shit hit the fan when I brought home an (gulp!)

American. In my family, you see, there are only *two* kinds of people—Italians and Americans (feared, lowly Americans). My mother was the ruler (make that Ruler), the *capo de tutti capi*. If she couldn't get you to do what she wanted through guilt, then she simply picked up the nearest and heaviest object at hand and belted you across the head. When I arrived home with my American fiancé, it was "you people, are you crazy?" From the screaming, fighting, and curses in my marriage that followed, I began to think she might be right.

My wedding took place in August 1969 and was a major event—a traditional Italian Catholic wedding, complete with curses. I went into the church on a beautiful sunny summer day and came out to a dark, rainy, and windy welcome. Was this an omen?

We left for our honeymoon at Niagara Falls and took the curses right along with us. The Falls was shut off for the first time in probably fifty years. I didn't even know they could do something like that. Niagara without the Falls isn't exactly an invitation to romance, so we did a quick tour and hightailed it to Mexico for what was to be the start of a very unglamorous part of my life.

My new husband was an alcoholic Vietnam vet who spent many of his waking hours and most of his sleeping ones reliving the horrors of war. I felt a long way from what had seemed like the friendly skies. Three daughters later and after years of hiding this terrifying, crazy life from outside eyes, I asked the question that many wives have asked before and since: "How the hell did I get here?" I attempted to find the humor in my situation, which particularly came in handy during my later career with MGM.

It may have been the "war zone" I lived in that prepared me for some truly awesome battles in the air. A few drinks during dinner at a restaurant and my husband would just slip away. Pity our fellow diners if an Asian walked in. I'd watch bemused as the father of my daughters would flip the table over and yell, "Duck, hit the ground," pushing us under the table for protection. The bad news was that the management saw less humor in the situation than I did. The good news was that we seldom had to pay for a meal.

As the years combined to form a decade, there were separations, reconciliations, more separations, and attempts at making peace. He was the quiet, unhappy, troubled husband. I was the crazy, assertive, nagging wife in a textbook dysfunctional family.

I spent years fooling myself by thinking, *When he stops drinking . . . when he's over Nam,* while focusing on dealing with the daily problems and crises. And then, when the drinking suddenly stopped, I actually expected my life to change and all the bad days to be over.

But the hell at home was far from over. For one of my children, it started in junior high and got progressively worse—depression, drinking, and suicidal threats. There were doctors, therapy, support groups, and fighting the disease of alcoholism all over again.

After years of marriage, being a mom, working at one boring job after another, I began to think more and more about flying and once again went looking for a way to get back to the sky. Is it any wonder that a job offer with MGM Grand Air was too tempting to walk away from? It meant escape, if only for a day at a time.

At the time I interviewed with MGM Grand Air, I was forty years old. My daughters were just turning seventeen, fourteen, and seven. Not great ages for Mom to be gone a lot, but I felt I had to do something for me, to allow me to feel good about myself again. Of course I didn't know at the time that working with the spoiled rich and famous, in addition to some terrible management, would threaten exactly the self-esteem I was seeking.

Travel was something that financially had been impossible until now. My problems had been with me for more than half my life and would not go away despite my best efforts. Controlling the choices my family made was beyond me, and I felt like a failure as wife and mother.

The kind of opportunity for travel, excitement, and everything else offered by this job with MGM Grand Air comes only once in a lifetime. I agonized over the decision to accept a job that would take me away from those who needed me most. Even then, for all its pluses, I knew taking to the skies wasn't without its negative side. Finally I made my decision and refused to let the opportunity pass me by. My husband, as any man might, became insecure when his wife began to travel the world, surrounded by the rich and infamous. The ongoing pressures of my new job drove the wedge between us deeper. Yet, this was my time. My moment to shine. And I vowed not to let a second of the excitement slip through my fingers or toes.

When your loved ones are killing their pain with outside help (alcohol or drugs), you go through surgery daily without the anesthesia. How many times I would leave for a flight after either a fight with my daughter or husband, or a wrenching session with the therapist. I would cry all the way to the airport, fix my face in the restroom, and then walk onto the stage known as the flight deck beaming defiantly, ready for the next adventure of life.

No way in hell would I ever bring my problems on that plane. I didn't have the time! My coworkers were my best therapy and biggest support group. Some of my coworkers became my "kids" and I would do whatever I could to help them. I would try to leave my problems on the tarmac and lose myself in their problems and in dealing with the numerous problems a celebrity clientele entails. My coworkers started calling me Mom. I had other nicknames that matched other aspects of my personality, however. Hot and wicked singer Freddie Jackson gave me the name Dirty Diana after experiencing my personalized safety demo. I also became known as Fag Hag and protector of gays, so labeled by the resident homophobics.

If my coworkers were my support, our celebrity passengers became my distraction, my escape from reality. I found it amazing that I would spend my days meeting and melding with superstars, lay over in places I never thought I'd see, and get propositioned more times than my diary had pages. I was told to expect the unexpected, the intolerable, the fantastic. Yet, every difficult passenger was a breeze compared to what awaited me at home or what I had just left behind. The fact that I was twice the age of most of my coworkers just made me feel I had more to prove.

I had heard talk referring to the senior flight attendants as the Flintstones—that they were slow, not pulling their weight. As it turned out, most complaints by passengers were about the young flight attendants, not the seniors. Our regulars wanted and requested us. I worked the hardest positions on the plane, dealt with the most demanding or difficult passengers, carried and set up the heaviest tables. I would always try to do the work of two and ran instead of walking. I was determined no one could say I was a slacker.

From the time I was a young girl, I had always enjoyed making people laugh, and now the aisle of a Boeing 727 was my stage. The more out of control my personal life became, the more daring my routines would become in flight. I found no one too intimidating or difficult. I never experienced the star awe so many of the others did in flight.

Some girls were tongue-tied and powerless when

they had someone like Tom Cruise on board. To me, intimidation was your kid throwing your mistakes at you. Awe was directed at the cruelty and manipulation used by those you loved. What could be the more perfect background to handle athletes and rock stars? If you could raise kids, then you had a shot at dealing with these adult children.

I'm happy to say all my passengers survived, and my three girls, well, they survived, too. They are beautiful (inside and out), bright, independent, and, most important, funny young women. Humor is the quality we share. Did I say humor? Hell, where the passengers of MGM Grand were concerned, it was more like a comedy of arrogance coupled with undeflatable egos. And all encouraged by an airline that prided itself on its eagerness to do everything necessary to keep its famous passengers satisfied—with a capital S(ex).

2 THE AIRLINE

In September 1987, MGM Grand Air was conceived as a luxury carrier created solely to cater to the transportation needs of the wealthy and celebrated. It was the brainchild of Kirk Kerkorian, himself a billionaire and a very big deal.

Kerkorian knew what the rich expected from an airline and intended to make certain they weren't disappointed. Three 727s were gutted and transformed into the ultimate in opulence, designed to carry thirty-five passengers in a space that Boeing originally meant to carry three times that amount.

From champagne to caviar to individually prepared entrees, MGM Grand was prepared to cater to its guests' every whim. The travel experience began when passengers were picked up in stretch limousines from their homes or hotels and taken to private terminals and lounges at airports in Los Angeles and New York. These two cities served as the hubs for MGM Grand, although later charter service would send us around the world.

The rich and famous were among their own kind, flying, wining (and whining), and dining with their peers. The in-flight service consisted of three hours of food and beverage served on tables covered with linen, fine china, imported crystal, and silver. Footstools were provided to keep royal toes from ever hitting the floor, as flight attendants raced fore and aft in an effort to satisfy ever-increasing demands.

The flight attendants chosen to start this airline were handpicked through a series of exhausting interviews. Of the more than five hundred original applicants, fewer than sixty were finally chosen. The combination of a few experienced flight attendants with eager, attractive, and inexperienced new personnel guaranteed that passengers would be pampered by both youth and knowledge. MGM wanted us to create our own special brand of service.

At least that was the plan. And to a great extent that was the illusion maintained through much of the airline's seven-year run (which included both scheduled and charter service). As is often the case in show business, the reality of our situation was quite different from the passengers' perception of it. As they sank into their velour bucket seats and wondered if their champagne would be chilled to perfection, we were busy in the back of the aircraft saying a silent prayer that the plane would hold together for another cross-country flight.

We nicknamed our 727s based on their individual mechanical problems. Aircraft 502 was called Deathstar, for we would always wonder if we were going to make it to our destination. On several occasions, an engine would have to be shut down for one reason or another. And there were always unexplainable thumps and bangs in the rear of the aircraft, though never in the same place twice. Yet Deathstar flew every trip like the old veteran she was, always managing to limp back home to her hangar amid the very vocal sighs of relief from the crew.

Aircraft 503 was dubbed Breathless because of her rapid decompressions. I don't know why, but Pee-Wee Herman always seemed to be on Breathless a lot. I'm sure there's no connection.

We called 504 Lady Dare because of all her "inop" stickers. Those are the little self-stick notices pasted across the cockpit and other parts of the aircraft judged to be inoperable equipment. Lady Dare was always daring us to fly her just once more—a dare we never failed to take.

When I first started to fly, I knew no fear. By the time I reentered the ranks of flight attendants, I was a working mother and things were different. It didn't help that the final hug and kiss from my little girl was accompanied by her cry, "Call if you crash." The jump seat became the equalizer for me, the crucial moments in which to review my evacuation commands and procedures. I listened to the sounds of our planes during takeoff and landing as a new mother listens to her sleeping infant.

The planes were rattletraps, yet our select mechanics were magicians and our pilots miracle workers. Each did his best to get us home, and they did—every single time. Being a natural worrier, I couldn't help but wonder why security wasn't tighter. On each flight, we carried million-dollar athletes, superstars, and rock groups—high-visibility targets for hijackings and ransom. *Amazing,* I thought. I wouldn't book my entire family on a single plane, let alone fly the entire L.A. Lakers or Chicago Bulls on the same plane.

We were a small group subjected to the vulgarities of the executives in charge. We quickly peeled off into cliques—new vs. old, tramps vs. scamps, rock fuckers (who turned some rock charters into flying bordellos) vs. career crews (who took their jobs seriously). There were the athletic fuckers (who worked to maintain their macho images) vs. the gays, the lick click (young women) vs. the bedrocks (seniors), the butt kissers vs. the independents. The list went on and on.

At MGM Grand Air, the politics, games, and gossip carried into the layovers and off time. A larger company would have had a corporate policy. At MGM, the only policy was no policy, as we were subjected to the "different strokes for different folks" mentality of the management. Who you blew, whether among management or passengers, won out over what you knew time after time as a lot of good people fell by the wayside.

Young or old, gay or straight, male or female, there was one thing that united us all. Somehow, when you stepped aboard our fleet of aging aircraft, the SEX AVAIL-ABLE sign flashed overhead (or, at least, in our passengers' heads). As the passengers cruised the flight attendants and each other, the flight attendants did their best to remain unaffected by the wall-to-wall celebrity show around us.

It wasn't really as hard to ignore as it sounds, considering what a typical flight required from each of us. We all greeted the passengers at the door as they boarded. They were individually escorted to their seat. As we turned to leave, we would do our best to convince them that we were not deserting them, but rather would come back to take their coats, bags, and other carryons.

The rich had a delicious way of looking right at us and ignoring everything we'd just said. In this case, they would immediately throw everything they were carrying in our direction. By the time we finally had everyone seated, we were so loaded down with heavy wraps, furs, leather jackets, and sport coats that trying to remember what belonged to whom was a challenge in itself. We tried to smile, all the while looking as if we were carrying our firstborn as we attempted to walk with this load.

How I loved when a female passenger would order me to take her wrap. More times than I care to admit, I'd slip and tell her: "Sure. Just call anytime you want to borrow it." (Well, she told me to take it!) I'd always get the look. You know the one. Like they just bit down on a rotten nut and weren't sure whether to swallow or spit out.

On other occasions, I just couldn't stop myself if female passengers were wearing something really great. I'd ask them to call me if they ever had a garage sale. (Bill Cosby's wife always laughed at the line, but she never called.) Sometimes we'd look at all the expensive furs in that closet and comment, "Well, someone's giving great head." Yes, we were a sick lot.

Next, there was the challenge of dealing with all the on-board luggage. Our passengers all packed as if they were relocating permanently to New York, instead of flying there for just a couple of days. Samsonite doesn't make as many bags as some of these stars own. And heavy bags at that. I often thought we were flying a planeload of Jeffrey Dahmers. There had to be bodies packed in those bags.

As any seasoned traveler knows, the best way to pack for a short trip is a small carry-on bag with toiletries, medicines, and a few pieces of mix-and-match clothing. Obviously, the concept was too simple to apply in real life—or as real as the lives of these passengers ever got.

I once asked David Copperfield if he could make his carryon disappear as he sat on his tight little ass watching me trying to lift it. Did he offer to help me with it? No. (Nor did he have a sense of humor about it.)

The airplane closet was packed with carry-on bags, which we would have to move four times per flight. Unlike more conventional carriers, we didn't have overhead or under-seat room for storage. How I'd dread having to go back into that closet to try and find that one bag a passenger just had to have "right now." With my tight, short skirt riding up to God knows where, I'd reach into that closet, struggling with the bags, only to end up losing my balance and falling in. My legs would be dangling out into the aisle. I'd be there stuck, my skirt nearly over my head. Trying to wiggle free, I'd feel a hand on my ass. *Help is here,* I'd think. But no, he was just making sure I didn't get up while he was stepping over me to get to the lav.

I suppose some people would say that we wanted the job and that petite female bodies should have no problem moving around bags weighing more than fifty pounds, but saying doesn't make it so and we're just not made that way. I was always amazed when passengers would bring on bags they could barely drag. If a 185- to 250-pound man has to pay a baggage carrier to bring his bag on board, what the hell made him think we 100- to 130-pound women could now carry it? We would stand at the door of the plane and watch with dread and disgust as they headed our way. They would take one step on board and drop it at our feet.

After the first year of grunge duty taking the carry-ons, I realized either my back wouldn't last much longer or I'd end up one day stepping over my uterus in the aisle. I finally learned to tell passengers, "If the bag is too heavy for one of us, you can either carry it to the closet yourself, or we can have it checked in for you.

This is a nonstop flight. The chances of it getting lost are next to nothing."

The rich and famous would rather part with their eldest son than their bags. No one liked the options but most understood—most but not all. One of the few who raised a stink and absolutely refused to act like a gentleman (or even a human) was Brian Grazer. The well-known Hollywood producer who is partnered in Imagine Films with Ron Howard thought he was divine, or something, and absolutely refused to go along with the choices offered. He boarded, dropped his bag at my feet, and wouldn't carry it to the closet or let it go into the belly.

Now, I'm as eager to be discovered as the next person and never look to piss off the powerful in any case, but principle is principle and my aching back was not about to allow me to give in. Truth is, I couldn't have carried (and would have had a hell of a time even dragging) his bag.

I tried to explain the situation to him and even apologized that I couldn't carry it. Mr. Grazer took the low road and totally ignored me. So, bitch that I am and a quart low on estrogen, I had his bag taken off the plane. His reaction? Do the words "shocked" and "pissed" say anything? Ah, Hollywood. He did get over it, because I catered to him for the entire flight to New York. See, you can make lemonade out of lemons.

If our backs didn't break because of the baggage, turbulence usually did the job. We would be out in the aisle working when, without any warning, the plane would hit an air pocket and send us slamming into a partition, a seat, the bar, the floor, or the ceiling. (I hit the ceiling once so hard that two full hours later I felt I'd been in a car wreck.)

With our bar loaded down with wine, champagne bottles, and fine crystal, we'd start bouncing. We crawled to the bar, becoming body shields between flying glass and screaming passengers. I'm sure they thought we were trying to save the booze and stemware. Quite honestly, we merely didn't want our passengers hurt. The paperwork alone was a bitch to complete.

Of course, when possible, the cockpit would warn us. We would try to prepare by stowing the potentially dangerous item. We could be rocking 'n' rolling in the sky, and our lovely drunks would still insist on being up. Most times, we would push these macho superstars back into their seats and buckle their asses down, just so we could be thrown to the floor instead.

One flight that is seared in my memory managed to take out three of us on a flight to L.A. We were working the back of a DC-8. Just as we were finishing up our service with freshly baked cookies, we hit some nasty turbulence and rode the flight from hell. The newer flight attendants on duty with me were preparing to follow me down the aisle with the beverage and milk trays. Our captain had warned us of some suspected turbulence and suggested that we use plastic instead of the usual crystal glasses.

Our first trip down the aisle was bumpy, but nothing we hadn't dealt with before. I went to the galley to replenish the cookie tray and went back out to the aisle. Just then, we were hit again. Hard and fast. One minute I was in the aisle with a tray of chocolate chip delights, the next I was headed for the ceiling. Cookies crushed against me, the wall, and eventually the floor, where I landed with a thud.

The poor flight attendant in front of me was on her way to the floor, leaving passengers wearing milk with their cookies. At least there was no glass. As I came back down from my trip to the ceiling, a large black man reached out and attempted to pull me onto the empty seat next to him. Unfortunately, the turbulence was too strong, and back up and down I went. Finally, my black knight was successful as I slammed my bottom into the armrest. I'd given birth to three children through natural childbirth, but nothing, *nothing* came close to the experience of landing on that armrest.

Being the lady I was and not having the highest threshold for pain, I heard "Oh fuck me" pass my lips (now where had I picked that up?). The big black man said, "Maybe later." Probably wanted to wait until things smoothed out some. My mind was racing. Dear God, why wasn't my ass home watching soaps and eating bonbons? I was too old for this.

My friend in the aisle was still in trouble, and I yelled for her to drop to the floor—as if she could do anything else. I crawled out to help her, thrusting one arm in her direction while holding on to my seat with the other. The noise from the galley was unreal. Cabinets opened, carriers flew, glass broke and joined the silver that was now everywhere.

Fortunately, one of our deadheading flight engineers was en route to the galley and flight attendant number three. He went to rescue the poor girl, last seen holding on to the bottom of a curtain and sliding from one end of the galley to the other. She was bloody, bruised, covered with trash, and probably wondering why no one mentioned this part in her interview.

If turbulence was the rugged part of the job, onboard pets were the easiest. I'm a real pet lover, and I thought it was great when stars would think enough to bring Rover or Coo-Coo or Bridget aboard to be babied like any other paying passenger. Actually, I got far more satisfaction bringing a dog or cat an ice cube to lick than I did from dealing with its owner. Well, except for the dog that sent back the paté and requested sorbet instead. The dog had his own place at a stateroom table. He wasn't really a bad passenger, though it was one of the times I didn't appreciate a passenger's wet kiss good-bye. Michael J. Fox, Jennifer Grey, Mary Tyler Moore, Joan Rivers, Elizabeth Taylor, and Ms. Slap Your Face Gabor traveled with their pets. It was quite common to see an entire stateroom (or, in Ms. Moore's case, more than one) paid for and reserved strictly for pets.

And on the subject of animals, the rich and famous men aboard would love to ask us "hired help" for a footstool, just to see us on our knees. Often, while down there on the floor, I'd mumble just loud enough to be heard, "Don't even think about grabbing the back of my head." They'd either laugh or wonder if they'd heard correctly.

Soon after, it was time to set up the tables. No drop-down trays here. Far too simple. On MGM Grand, everyone ate at an actual table that latched on to the side wall. While each felt as if it weighed a ton, in actuality each table tipped the scale at around twenty pounds, which in midair feels like a ton in any case. No matter how we struggled and huffed, no one ever deemed to offer assistance.

After setting up the tables, it was time to take meal and drink orders. It's amazing how many passengers would refuse to answer when we asked them something as simple as "Would you care for wine with your dinner?" Hired help I was, but a mind reader I wasn't. "Wine?" I'd ask again. Even the obvious drunks would just stare back speechless with a look that suggested they were attempting to solve a calculus equation. It didn't seem to matter how well heeled or well known our passengers were, they all seemed to take leave of common courtesy somewhere between the terminal and their barrel seats. They seemed to have left their brains as well.

One thing that always seemed to stump the well heeled were the headsets. Time after time those old call buttons would ring so wildly that you were certain you were being called to perform CPR. The big emergency:

"Miss, these headsets don't work." The headset cord would inevitably be dangling in plain sight at their feet. While our smiling lips would always say the prescribed comeback—"Oh, let me check them for you"—our minds would be thinking, *Let's plug them in, dummy.*

It would also never fail that when the rich and famous were offered a tray of cookies, they would find it necessary to ask, "Which are the chocolate chip?" Please, I've never known children to have a problem with finding the right ones.

Speaking of kids, there is no controlling the off-spring of someone who is rich. I have seen better behaved kids on parole than these spoiled little tykes. They weren't born with just a silver spoon in their mouths but also with a stick of dynamite up their asses. Food fights among teens were an almost daily event. The cleaners would come on, and we would just stand back and watch their faces. Anything that was served or discarded on board was on the floor, seats, and walls— crushed cookies, food, and even used diapers.

Don't get me started on diapers. It was common to be handed a shit-filled diaper. Not wanting to take the time to go into the lav and change that child, the very rich chose to do it on the spot at their plush velour seats. Never mind that the smell would be through the entire cabin within seconds. Never mind that others were eating. So what would they do with that stinky, caca-filled mess? They'd stash it in some little crevice— the theory being, I suppose, that someone would find it after they left the plane. If the cleaning crew missed it, we would find it midway through the next flight, usually after an unsuspecting passenger would reach between the seats for a dropped pen. The innocent traveler would get this blank look of disbelief on his face, and who could blame him?

I actually got pretty good at going blank myself, particularly when dealing with an obnoxious passenger. One evening on a flight from New York, I was serving four executives in a stateroom. They were in deep conversation, yet courteous enough to me. All, that is, except for one.

He began to snap his fingers and point every time he wanted more champagne. Suddenly I found myself neither hearing nor seeing (or pretending not to at least) each time he did his snap-and-point routine. After several unsuccessful attempts to get my attention, he finally lost all patience and grabbed my arm.

"Listen, honey, if you take care of me, I'll take care of you," he slurred. Now there was a line this woman was going to believe! All the men in the stateroom stopped talking, waiting for my reply. I didn't disappoint them. I looked Mr. Obnoxious in the eye and said, "Looks like we're both gonna have a long wait, huh, honey?"

Mostly by choice, as I enjoyed interacting with the passengers, I always seemed to be serving Mr. Obnoxious or another of his kind. The in-cabin crew consisted of five flight attendants. The lead flight attendant, called either the in-flight service manager or purser, would take meal orders and movie requests, arrange for limos, and work with the food and beverage specialist (a.k.a. galley slave) to get the meals served up and handed to the flight attendants in the aisle. Since the galley slave worked overtime just preparing and cooking the meals to order, this left only three flight attendants in the aisle to service thirty-five passengers. I chose to be out there in the aisle in the thick of the action, not missing a thing.

Doesn't sound that difficult, huh? Join me on the front line. You've invited thirty-five of your most important business associates over for cocktails and dinner. Two of your friends have volunteered to help—one of them worthless or clueless. Among your treasured guests: a drunk couple, maybe four or more on coke, a good half-dozen who won't acknowledge you, a couple more fucking in the bathrooms, and at least eight more who shouldn't be out without a keeper—all will be clamoring for attention.

Your assignment, if you haven't already hidden your head in the sand, is to serve five to seven courses, replenish beverages and silverware, answer questions, send faxes, bring phones, find bags, turn on televisions, adjust headsets, make cappuccinos, prepare beds, remake beds, and check and clean the bathrooms (every fifteen minutes). Now do all this during an earthquake and two tremors (equivalent to turbulence), and have the whole house cleaned up as if nothing ever happened within three-and-a-half to four hours.

Damn, I forgot to tell you to strap weights around your ankles to account for the pull on your body. (Your job is a little easier than a deep-sea diver's.) And, by all means, never forget to smile at all times, to ignore the sweat pouring down your body, and to pretend you don't know your face is on your blouse collar. Your bladder is screaming "Stop and pee *now*," your feet are screaming "Your shoes just shrunk two sizes," your skirt is screaming "Get the Gas-X. We're gonna blow."

A male passenger slips you his business card, and you smile and look flattered when all you really care about is that now maybe he'll stop hitting the call button. While you're running your ass off to get everything done on time, you are still building rapport, flirting, playing ambassador, dealing with the anonymous male hand that slips up your leg when you bend over—all the time observing the inner dynamics on board and the various games being played, not to mention one or two fights you must break up along the way.

After all are fed, bottled, and burped, it is time to turn on the electronic babysitter—the movie. More fights. Some actors don't want their movie played on their flights. Others insist on it. Luckily we had quite the collection of films aboard—all the better to adapt.

Hey, where did you go? Oh, you're down on all fours looking for something. No doubt the glamour. If you find it, let me know.

3 THE CREW

Fascinating celebrities and exciting travel were certainly a large part of my MGM Grand experience. Yet, the most important perks were the friends I made—the ones who will always be part of my life, and the ones I lost to death. Ironically, some of the characters I worked with are more lasting in my memories than the celebs. For the most part, our famous passengers were far too busy to notice their crews because they had their heads up their asses. With this glimpse at the behind-the-scenes crew, perhaps now they, too, will have a second chance to see what they missed.

❀ Ms. Jenny the Juicer ❀

She was one of my oldest friends at MGM, and how I loved Jenny (nicknamed the Juicer because of her penchant for fresh fruits and vegetables). We met the first day of training. Since both of us had to drive from East

Fuck to be at class in L.A., she asked if I was interested in sharing a hotel room. Given my gasoline bill and my need to economize, it made sense, until I realized that while both she and I and several other girls in the room knew about our arrangement, the hotel did not. We actually pulled off the subterfuge for weeks—or at least we did until the shower incident.

One of the women was in the shower, when suddenly the shower head blasted loose and smacked her square on the forehead. Thanks to her screaming and the subsequent flooding, security was sent up to our room. I barely had time to hide under the bed. While you don't have to be forty to feel foolish hiding under a bed, I was and did. Jenny took the entire incident in stride, and I must admit I was hooked on our friendship in the spirit of adventure alone.

Everyone in class looked upon us as the odd couple. There I was, a smoking, drinking, truck driver–talking woman. There she was, prim and proper, not to mention a natural beauty. While I would put anything down my throat (and did), Jenny existed mainly on the flesh of fruits and vegetables, which she peeled constantly throughout the day. They cost her nearly nothing, so little in fact that we always said that she could write a book titled *Europe on Less Than Fifty Cents a Day.*

This was one woman with talent. The way she ate a banana alone was so sexual she could stop traffic. (In fact, she did just that on a number of occasions.) I loved carpooling with her. If and when we were stuck in traffic on the freeway, she would just whip out her banana and the truck drivers would give her the road.

This girl was not a gagger. I was amazed at how far she could take that fruit down her throat. Finally I asked how she got so good. She told me that she practiced sucking a tennis ball through a garden hose. I think she was kidding, but then with Ms. Jenny, you just never really knew for sure. There was a split second I actually considered trying a garden hose, but then wondered just how I would explain the exercise to my three daughters.

"Mom, what are you *doing*?"

Or God forbid that I actually *managed* to suck that ball through the hose and it lodged in my throat. I'd make the news: "Mother of Three, Gagged by Tennis Ball, Found Clutching a Garden Hose."

While everyone else went along with her Juicer nickname, I personally preferred to call her Ms. Clean. She was never without her can of Lysol spray (all the better to disinfect those wonderful hotel rooms we stayed in). The Lysol was joined in her purse by a paring knife and an assortment of much too large zucchini, yams, and fruit. Don't think for one moment that I believed they were strictly for dietary purposes. I always wanted to check them out and see where the hell she stuck those "D" batteries into them.

While her diet was supposed to be healthy, it sure didn't do much for her energy level. Ms. Clean was one of the few slam-clickers among the crew—slam-clickers meaning those who would enter their hotel rooms, slam the doors, and then click the dead bolts for the night.

I kept telling her to get out and have a steak, a drink, a cigarette, and a good lay—in that order, knowing full well that she would feel a lot better. After all, it certainly worked for the other flight attendants. One thing I have to admit, her diet did keep her very slim. And why not? What went into that girl came out immediately. No wonder she had no energy to party.

It was only after the Federal Aviation Administration had banned smoking completely on domestic flights that I learned a new fact about my friend. I kept smelling something burning and made myself crazy sniffing through the cabin. I knew no one was in the lav sneaking a smoke. (Hell, *I* wasn't in the lav sneaking a smoke!)

I couldn't figure it out and finally went to another flight attendant. She started laughing and pulled me into the forward closet. Apparently, our little gal was having a real problem with gas that day. She was sneaking into the closet, cutting loose, and lighting matches to cover up the aroma. She was afraid she would set off the smoke detector in the lav and this was her ladylike solution. Well, what are friends for? I told her where to cut loose . . . there's 5B, 10A, 14B, etc. "Honey, don't waste this talent. Share it with the assholes on board."

❀ Mi Amico ❀

Mi Amico was my handsome Italian gay bud from Buffalo. Our resident Robert Downey, Jr., look-alike, he was constantly asked for his autograph when we were out in L.A. or New York. Whenever the announcement came for us to "cross-check" the doors before departure, he'd yell to me to "kick 'em over, girl." I'd oblige Mi Amico by sliding my high heels in his direction before yelling back, "Cross-check, dear, not cross-dress!" He did manage to stretch out my snug-fitting heels, though.

We were so close and so alike in speech, humor, and mannerisms that it was rumored by MGM that we were one and the same. "You'll never see them in the aisle at the same time." He also insisted that his legs were better than mine. I would never admit that he might be right.

He worked the galley and was a great chef. As a typical Italian, he wanted to make sure my kids had enough to eat and would push care packages on me to take home. I finally told him the Brownie troop leader had called and said the troop wasn't fond of the caviar. What did seven-year-olds know, anyway?

Very often we would fight and compete for the same passenger's attention. I'd say, "He gave me his number." He'd brag, "He asked for mine." I'd come back with, "Well, he grabbed my hand." Mr. One-Up would say, "Girlfriend, he grabbed my ass."

Remember I said he looked like Robert Downey, Jr.? Well, it was quite a sight when my look-alike friend actually got to cater to the original in flight. They both seemed to be quite taken with each other. Hmmm . . .

To this very day, he insists that he saved my life—

albeit long distance. We had just returned from a trip to New York. While he went right back out on the next flight East, I became really sick. It was one of those things that comes on quickly and knocks you for a loop. Unfortunately, I was stricken on the eve of a giant move. Knowing that I couldn't afford to be sick, I immediately took a couple of antibiotics when I got home and chased them down with a knock-out pill. The room was spinning just before I crashed and burned in bed. I was out.

He claims that he called and spoke to me on the phone, saying that I sounded depressed. Being a concerned friend and a dramatic Italian, he called back later to check on me. My daughter told him I was sleeping, had taken some pills, and was out like an old rock. My hero, my rescuer, my friend interpreted that as an admission that I had tried to kill myself. He screamed at my daughter from 3,000 miles away to call 911.

No fool she, my daughter attempted to explain that I was sick, but instead of listening, Mi Amico again screamed to call 911. Why my daughter chose this time to do what she was told I have never understood. I still think that in the back of her mind there was a little payback involved. Whatever the reason, the next thing I knew I was being awakened by the sound of fire trucks, sirens, cops, and paramedics. For a second, I thought I was hallucinating, only to later realize that I wasn't floating, but rather was being carted out of my home on a stretcher.

All the while, I was convinced this entire event was one hell of a dream. And why not? I had never been on a stretcher before. It wasn't until I was in the ambulance and on my way to the damn hospital that I fully comprehended what was happening.

It took twenty-four hours for me to convince everyone, including my doctor, that I was fine. To this day, my friend insists that he rescued me. At least I know he cares, but he doesn't have to laugh quite so much about it. With friends like these . . . I owe him one, but I'm not sure what.

❀ Imelda ❀

Imelda was the lovely and good-natured Asian flight attendant who was the brunt of my practical jokes. Her attempts at American slang coupled with her love of gambling helped her end up the lucky one who married a passenger. It was a coup for the senior flight attendants that it happened to one of us and not some brand new, young, and firm girl. Imelda deserved it more than anyone. She had raised a son on her own, had worked hard, and was just finishing paying for his college education.

She kept us all laughing at her naiveté, which was absolutely charming. It also begged to be tested, and I obliged as often as possible. While the episodes were many, a certain birthday prank does linger in my mind. We were being briefed before a flight at Los Angeles International Airport, and since it was Imelda's birthday, we all took time out to celebrate. In addition to singing "Happy Birthday," I gave her a gift—a very, very large vibrator.

Being the clever Italian that I am, I found this particular item in a very seedy little sex shop in Anaheim. (And you thought the city was famous only for Disneyland.) In any case, Imelda was surprisingly pleased by the gift, though certainly a little shocked at its size. As she carefully packed it in her carry-on bag, I assured our naive little coworker that she needn't worry about getting the gift through security since I had already gotten it through several times unnoticed. She believed me. Amazing.

After our flight to New York, Imelda disappeared with her present and didn't reappear until it was time for our return trip to Los Angeles the next day. She had a relaxed and radiant look about her that morning, and with a wink I complimented her on her rosy complexion, hardly able to contain myself.

When we arrived at the airport, I slipped away to have a private little chat with security, and later hid behind a partition to watch my plan hatch before my eyes. I saw Imelda casually walk up to the X-ray machine and place her bag on the belt with those of the surrounding passengers and crew.

As Imelda's bag went into the X-ray machine, the security girl peered at the screen and then called her supervisor. Imelda started to turn red and attempted to make small talk, to little avail. Security was playing out their role perfectly, and it had cost me only two decks of cards, two pens, and a handful of wings.

Poor Imelda looked sheepishly at the passengers with whom she would be trapped for the next four hours, panic written all over her face, as security announced loud enough for everyone to hear that she would have to empty her bag. (My God, those security girls were really good.)

Imelda resorted to begging and finally blurted out in her wonderful accent: "Please, no, don't open the bag," even as the uniformed guards were reaching into the suitcase. Much too loud she said, "You don't understand. It's a gag gift. It's a dildo."

The security girl, fearing she would crack under pressure, handed Imelda her bag back, pointing to me. I was peeking out from behind the wall and broke into a run to the plane. When she finally did board the plane, I apologized through my laughter, all the while assuring her that the passengers didn't see a thing. I then spent the first half of the flight telling as many passengers as I could. Poor dear Imelda. I can't give her enough credit for her good nature.

Making her all the more wonderful to tease was her adorable way of fracturing English. I remember on one of her flights, a boarding passenger commented to her that she was "a sight for sore eyes." The comment made her feel so good that she decided to share it with one of our regulars, Mr. Oh. She ran up to him and actually uttered the words, "Mr. Oh, you make my eyes hurt."

Imelda was one in a million.

❀ Leilani ❀

Imelda thought she had some embarrassing moments in flight, but they were nothing compared to our beautiful Hawaiian flight attendant, Leilani. It was a full flight to New York as Leilani was boarding passengers, stowing their carryons, and hanging up coats. She knew that an FAA representative was on board, checking out the cabin crew, so she was being extra cautious with her behavior. There would be no screwing around that day—not with that guy watching our every move.

Unfortunately, just as the safety demo was about to begin, Leilani had to pee in a wicked way. She had been holding off for the entire boarding process and now found herself between a rock and a hard place. Unable to wait another moment, she hurried to take care of business. She was just starting to feel relief when the safety demo began.

She pulled up her panty hose and dashed down the aisle to her position at midcabin. Flawlessly she went through the safety demo. Now the center of attention, she pivoted to point out the emergency exits on each side of the plane. Quite pleased with her performance, she took a deep breath, only to notice the FAA man smiling in her direction.

"Sorry," she said, thinking he might have noticed that she joined the demo midway through. "I was in the restroom. I just couldn't wait."

He looked up at her and answered, "That's okay. I

knew where you were. Your skirt is stuck in the top of your panty hose."

Poor Leilani, or as she was known from that moment forward, Sweet Cheeks. That will teach her not to wear underwear.

One flight a handsome gay purser and Leilani were in a deep and animated conversation. I asked, "What are you kids talking about?" He said, "Well, girlfriend here thinks I will go to hell because I sleep with men, and she says God wants me to try a woman." With this our Bible-toting girl said, "God spoke to me and said I need to save him from hell and stop his decadent life." She then grabbed his hand and placed it on my breast, telling him, "Here, feel the breast of a woman and you shall be saved." She just couldn't stop herself. It was a mission.

She made him squeeze my tit and he said, "I've been saved. I must have two of these. I think I'll start hormones tomorrow," and walked away. To which I added, "Oh shit, just get implants like the rest of the flight attendants." A disappointed Leilani said, "I just don't understand, it didn't work." I consoled her by saying, "Maybe God meant for him to feel your breast, dear." After this one I walked away saying my own prayer, "Thank you, God, for this job."

❀ Kujo ❀

Kujo is that flight attendant we've all known who has flown too many trips, been with too many airlines, and seen too much. Every airline has one and prays that she will either retire or somehow be swept off her feet and fly off into the sunset. But she never does, showing up instead with every start-up airline.

Kujo had a big heart and fought to the death for the fair treatment of the newest flight attendants. Yet, despite her positive efforts, this was one broad who managed to get on *everyone's* nerves. Just looking at her made me nervous. Perhaps it was that bad and obvious face-lift that gave a perpetual artificial grin. Whatever the reason, she glared, stared, and gave us plenty of reasons to feel uncomfortable and to avoid working with her.

Because Kujo knew her stuff, she was used to train the flight attendants and keep the FAA happy. She knocked herself out to get them through their mini-evacuation trials, drilling them relentlessly on the finer aspects of ditching. Whatever else I might say about her, she was probably the most capable flight attendant, and the one you would want to have on board in an emergency.

Yet, there was always that smile. Yuk. Unfortunately, whoever did her face-lift also seemed to have been involved with her liposuction and 1950s hairstyle as well. I remember one particular layover in Acapulco, when the crew were all sunbathing by the hotel pool. I was sitting next to a quiet but funny pilot whom we called Cowboy Bob. Kujo came down to join us. As she walked past us in her bathing suit, naturally we couldn't help but stare. One pilot said, "What was that?" Cowboy Bob responded, "I don't know, but somebody iron it."

Am I being crude? You tell me. Kujo's breast implants were put in so long ago that everyone swore they could see one slipping now and then. Or perhaps they were trying to explain away the fact that she was always discreetly trying to adjust her bra strap.

Then there was the Vaseline. She constantly applied the stuff to her face to ward off wrinkles. Did I say wrinkles? Her face was so shiny that even dirt couldn't stick to it. Kujo and her Vaseline were an inseparable pair. She never flew without it, and certainly didn't care if passengers saw her apply it. We'd joke that the cockpit and mechanics had to borrow her grease to help fix certain mechanical problems. If we ever had to evacuate that plane, we kidded that she would be thrown down the slide first to facilitate everyone else's escape.

She was prone to dramatic mood swings, which all of us associated with her lack of sex. The flight crews united to bribe potential suitors to accommodate her, including offering her up on the sex altar of the entire L.A. Clippers and Lakers basketball teams. Despite our best efforts, those sex gods took one look at Kujo and just shook their heads. (Even Gary Grant of the Clippers wouldn't take her on, and we thought he would do *anyone*.)

On one particular Lakers flight, I finally resorted to telling the boys that she liked it facedown with a pillow over the back of her head. The visual apparently got the better of them, for suddenly the entire plane was all smiles as Kujo walked by. Misinterpreting all the excitement directed toward her, Kujo took me aside and told me that she had decided to fly more often with the Lakers since they really seemed to like her. Backfire. Backfire, big time! Since I flew most of the Lakers and Clippers flights, now I was going to be stuck with Kujo as well.

It didn't take long before my little joke spread throughout the National Basketball Association teams like a California fire. No matter. The "facedown and pillow over her head woman" still didn't get lucky. Instead, a collection was taken up among crew members to hire a Hollywood makeup artist to concoct something that could be added to her Vaseline that once applied would give her some color. A lot of effort went into this special project, but we were never able to accomplish our goal.

On one flight during which she had irritated the crew to the breaking point, they did take action—action usually reserved for only the very nastiest passengers. Visine was added to her bottled water. What? You don't know the Visine trick? A few drops added to any liquid and you get the runs for days. Poor Kujo. Although she never drank from her water bottle that evening on the van ride into town, apparently she did when she got back to the hotel. The next morning, she was unable to make the return flight home, and it was a scramble to replace her for the trip back to L.A.

Now don't get the impression that Kujo was a virgin or never got laid. A couple of our braver pilots resorted to taking care of the situation personally. Funny, I think I miss Kujo. I guess she had her good points, though they were often hard to see. Wherever you are, please sleep faceup, girl.

❀ Honey ❀

To talk about Honey is to talk about sex. While I wondered how to pay my bills, Honey's biggest challenge was deciding where her next orgasm was coming from. I was dumbfounded by the simplicity of this woman's life, and I secretly longed for a little of what she had.

I had to know more. Suddenly I couldn't pass a costume jewelry store without thinking, *Now I know who buys this stuff.* Honey, you see, had at least forty watches and the largest earrings an earlobe could hold. She had more wigs than Tammy Faye, and coats, jackets, vests, and purses made out of every animal imaginable.

I'd watch as she would pop pills for any imaginable reason—to lose weight, sleep, wake up, and have fun. She washed them all down with more alcohol than I would ever be able to consume and still live to tell about it the next morning. I was frustrated by her self-destruction, amazed by her zest for life, love, and lust, and impressed by her generous heart and spirit. The kind of woman who wouldn't hurt an insect, yet couldn't be kind to herself. She couldn't pass a homeless person without sharing. If the rest of us gave a dollar, Honey went home and cooked the person a meal and brought it back.

Honey is the perfect example of the sexually active MGM flight attendant. An affair with Jim (J.C.) Cleamons, then the Bulls' assistant coach, now head coach for Dallas, for eighteen months consisted of hotel liaisons on the road and in L.A. and Chicago. The affair ended mutually when J.C. started up with another flight attendant, a close friend of Honey's. It continued through his marriage and up to the writing of this book. J.C. would share his bed with the same flight attendant who also fit Bo Jackson into her busy schedule. Honey doesn't hold a grudge; after all, her friend gave her some great tickets for Lakers games after sleeping with Jerry West.

Honey seemed to be drawn to assistant coaches. Next came R.C., at that time of the L.A. Clippers. R.C. was a happily married little man who would fit two flight attendants into his busy schedule. Hey, they both had short red hair, maybe he didn't realize they were two different girls. And there was Jawaan Oldham, #54. That was his jersey number. Jawaan was a rookie when they met. Let's not forget former L.A. Raiders assistant coach Doug Wilkerson, now with the St. Louis Rams. He stood out in her mind because of his endowment and his penchant for very rough sex.

Since we didn't fly the football teams—oh, thank

God—I had to know how she had met him. Apparently, she went along with another flight attendant to the Los Angeles Airport Sheraton. She was accompanying Leilani, who just happened to be carrying on with Stu Lantz, the Lakers' announcer. Stu had pursued and finally worn down this girl. She had put in her time in hopes of a future. She was emotionally involved in the relationship. For Leilani it wasn't just celebrity sex. But he was an "honorable" man and wouldn't leave his wife. Doug Wilkerson was staying at the same hotel, so Leilani now introduced Honey to him. As the flight attendant went to rendezvous with Stu, Doug and Honey were left to their own devices. This was the beginning of their "for lust alone" affair.

Oh, let's not leave baseball out. There was Bobby Thigpen of the White Sox. How could she ignore this man? He, at least, offered chocolate-covered strawberries, champagne, and, by God . . . foreplay. Ah, he was quite the romantic. There was even country music playing in the background. This went on until he was traded to another team. Surprise, never even a phone call. He got traded and so did Honey.

Okay, we're not done yet with the list of sports figures. How about the former athlete and now sportscaster Jim Hill. Don't be shocked. Many more athletes asked and pursued Honey with lunches, dinners, and tickets. She would meet James Worthy and Magic for lunch—separately, dear. Michael Jordan invited her up to his penthouse suite on the road, but she couldn't figure out where she would fit in since his "on the road" girlfriend was there already.

Let's not forget the rock charters. Rahamlee, a horn player with the Phil Collins tour. Quick fingers. Shane, video producer on the Madonna tour. Then there was the Rod Stewart tour, another musician. Honey was the blond flight attendant in the bathroom stall with Duff of Guns N' Roses, sharing coke and screwing.

Honey, I hope you are always in my life, dear girl. It is for you that the lyrics "wild women do and they don't regret it" truly applies. Happy orgasms.

❀ Gary ❀

I had to include Gary because we were enemies for such a long time. What a waste. All the while I thought he was going out of his way to make the pilots and flight attendants miserable, but it wasn't true. He was just a perfectionist and expected everyone else to be, too. It took the death of a mutual friend and coworker from AIDS before we finally buried the hatchet. It was done in his honor, and we vowed to be and stay friends.

Just one story about Gary, and I promise it will be short. He was the supervisor on duty during one particular flight. I had come in early, checked in, and went outside for my usual smoke. It was the perfect window for Gary to lecture me about the hazards of nicotine.

First came the lecture on the physical dangers.

"Yes, Gary, I've heard all that, but I still enjoy it," was my reply.

Next, he went for vanity. "What about what it does to your skin and teeth?" he argued.

"Yes, I know. I don't give a shit, Gary," came my response.

"Well," he continued, "what about what men say about women who smoke?" he queried.

"Say? Say what?"

"It's like licking an ashtray?" he countered.

At this point, I had had enough and shot back, "Yeah, and you think a dick tastes good?"

Poor Gary. Beets have never been redder than his face. He stammered to reply . . . to say anything. When he finally did speak, he could only come back with, "Only you would say something like that," and stomped away.

When I shared the story with Captain Ed in the cockpit and got to the last line, he lost it. He actually laughed so hard he couldn't function. The passengers thought it was turbulence.

He proceeded to share it with everyone he flew with for weeks. It didn't help my relationship with Gary, but it still makes me smile. Gary and I worked together to push the AIDS ribbons I made to collect money for Project Angel Food in memory of our friend. We have since cried together at other funerals of comrades fallen to this virus. And, yes, we've kept our promise to each other.

❀ Pattee ❀

Pattee was the other loud Italian in our group, a Dirty Diana in the making and most definitely not to be confused with Little Miss Perfect. How this one ever sneaked past management and got on line, I'll never figure out. I looked at her and saw myself twenty years earlier. And it pissed me off to see my ass on her walking away.

I watched as Pattee grew from a wild, single, and always hungover reveler to a married, responsible woman with child. I looked at her and knew I had another daughter.

The turning point came when MGM started to provide service for the Golden State Warriors basketball team. After a night out with the players in San Antonio, Pattee found out what a lightweight I was with booze. Having said that, it's true that we had been drinking from the time we got to our room, straight through dinner, and later while barhopping with the boys. They were buying drinks and we danced, shot pool, and hit every bar on the River Walk with them.

Finally, in the wee hours of the morning, when the players poured us into a cab, I was barely functioning. Halfway to the hotel, the booze hit. I knew I was going to puke. Our cabdriver slammed on the brakes and dragged me to the side of the road. God forbid I lose it in the cab.

Pattee started screaming at him to keep his "fucking hands" off of me. Pulling me back in the cab, she consoled me with the line, "Don't worry, Mom. You'll be fine. He's not touching you anymore." Unfortunately, when that damn cabby stepped on the gas pedal, the Italian volcano erupted. Poor Pattee. She just couldn't believe what shot out and with what force. The look on her face had me laughing and vomiting at the same time.

The cabdriver was swearing and yelling, of course. Pattee held her ground, uttering those words that I remember so well: "Shut the fuck up and drive." Like I said, Dirty Diana in the making. I laughed more and vomited more.

By the time we got to the hotel, the cabdriver was making veiled threats, yelling, "Look at my cab. You must pay for this." Pattee gave him every penny she had, but he still wanted more. I remember being pulled out of the cab and dragged through the hotel lobby with Mr. Cabby on our heels.

He was yelling something in one language; she was screaming "Fuck you" in English; and the hotel security guards were after us all. A caravan of crazy people. With Olympic determination, Pattee was relentless in getting Mom tucked into her room. Finally, the moment of truth arrived. I was pushed inside and aimed at the toilet. In the background, I still heard Pattee screaming "Fuck you," and then finally a door slammed and all was quiet. Even hugging that toilet, I managed to laugh through my tears.

The two of us bid every trip we could back to San

Antonio after that and it was a replay—though more often than not, it was Pattee who ended up hugging the toilet, not me. She always seemed to have the shits or a hangover. I worked double to cover for her in flight and never cared because I owed her—big time.

Perhaps Pattee's most outrageous talent was her ability to get back at passengers who pissed her off. Since she was usually sporting a hangover, she always seemed to have the worst gas and had absolutely no problem sharing it with all of us. If the crew would complain, she would merely go out and find a victim among the passengers. There was always someone to get back at. She would serve the passenger across the aisle from the intended victim, and then as sexy as can be, just stick her ass in the air and fire away. Bull's-eye!

I marveled at her gall. She really didn't give a shit—just gas—and made Italians everywhere proud to call her one of our own. She was so beautiful that the passengers never really wanted to believe it came from her. They would look at their fellow travelers and start moving around uncomfortably in their seats. Her favorite in-flight pastime.

Yet of all the things I remember about Pattee, there is one statement she made that will always echo in my mind. The service had just been completed and four flight attendants were hanging out in the galley. The conversation turned to men as usual, and, just as usual, everyone had a gripe.

The married lover that couldn't get away. The player

that treated her like dirt. The actor that called and pursued her until he got his piece and then bailed. Pattee listened as the rest of us talked, and then came up with a thought.

"I have a novel idea," she said. "Why doesn't everyone just go home and fuck their own husbands or boyfriends instead of these assholes?" It got real quiet and everyone just stared at her. "Nah, never mind, forget it," she said.

❀ Our Pat ❀

Pat was about six feet, five inches tall in heels, with muscular arms and legs, large hands, a deep voice, an overly animated disposition, and a huge Adam's apple. Our very own transsexual. Our male passengers and athletes had a strange attraction for her. I think it was for the kink value alone. Another flight attendant asked her one day if she had undergone surgery, and I thought she was going to bury him. Touchy, touchy, for such a big woman. She seldom went out of her hotel room during layovers and seldom was seen out of uniform. I often wondered who hired our Pat, and why.

❀ Ghassan ❀

Ghassan, the Lebanese gentleman, would take it upon himself to watch over every female flight attendant and gave MGM the class it deserved. At the end of our flights into Los Angeles, we would drag our tired asses out to our cars and burn rubber to get home, but not this man. He would light up his omnipresent cigar and patiently wait until every female flight attendant was safely in her car.

It drove him to the wall when I would light up a cigarette on the street.

"Madame, they will think you are a woman of the night."

"Ghassan, I am a flight attendant. They won't be wrong."

How often he would lecture me on not taking a bath, but rather to shower in the hotels. ("You never know who's been in the tub.") And never go barefoot. ("You might catch something.") I tried to explain that if a flight attendant was to catch something in a hotel, it would not be from bare feet or bathing. He would take a puff of his cigar and ponder that one.

He prepared the finest snacks for us in our rooms and taught me the finer points of enjoying vodka and stogies. Despite the fact that my reputation for being a drinker was legend, it took Ghassan only one layover in New York to prove to himself what a lightweight I actually was.

He decided to take me around the world by having me sample a shot of everything. I was only too eager to oblige, and did. Somehow, I managed to keep it all together the entire way back to the hotel, or at least until I opened the door to my room. Where there was in reality only one bed, I managed to see three. Of course, I chose the wrong one and hit the floor. It was the best thing that could have happened, because the fall knocked me out. (Ghassan worked very hard on the return flight while I spent four hours hugging the toilet and running to the cockpit for oxygen. We all covered each other's asses.)

On one of his first attempts in the galley, he held up a filet mignon and looked at it with admiration. His timing couldn't have been better, for just as I passed, he uttered, "Nice piece."

Never missing a opening, I said, "Why, thank you." It was the least I could do.

He laughed and, ever the gentleman, said, "But, of course, Madame, I would be honored to fuck you."

I miss and worry about my Ghassan, who is back in his home city of Beirut. Ghassan, everyone misses you. Stay safe. I would be honored to fuck you, too.

❀ Body Beautiful, the African Princess ❀

There wasn't a male passenger who didn't look twice at this girl, the African Princess. They all wanted her, but she was not about to settle for anything less than the perfect man. She was a model and struggling actress, and when she wasn't out shopping for Mr. Right, she was making up one excuse after another to get out of work for an audition.

One day she was in a panic because she had a callback

for a part on a network soap opera. Unable to get time off, she actually showed up for her flight and revealed her tale of woe. Tossing her into the john, I went to the flight supervisor and explained that I couldn't possibly risk flying with anyone who was throwing up before a flight. The supervisor didn't think the passengers would like it either and said to tell her to go home. What's the big deal working short a crew member if she had a shot at her dream? And as it turned out, Miss Body Beautiful got the part.

I respect this girl because she did accomplish her goals by hard work alone. We were excited when she co-starred in a major film about a plane hijacking. And she still can be seen on television. There can be happy endings after all.

❀ Captain Ed ❀

Captain Ed was simply the best pilot I've ever known. I bid trips with him just to feel safe. Ed, known as our resident "Velvet Brick," was one very mysterious, horny, and cantankerous flyer. Former CIA and God knows what else, the good captain is mentioned in the book *Air America.* On his days off, he disappeared to unknown destinations. What a guy. We were drawn together because of our rebel don't-take-any-bullshit attitude.

On our first trip together, he jumped out of the crew van and went straight to his hotel room. We were all getting together to relax in the bar, so I went to his room and pounded on his door. He opened it up wearing only a towel and an expression on his face that gave new meaning to the phrase *if looks could kill.*

Undaunted, I just looked up at him and said, "Get the fuck down to the bar and join us." Breaking out with a smile, he said, "Okay." I knew I was right about him. Just a big old teddy bear inside—well, at least with us girls.

Captain Ed also held the record for asking me to sit on his face the most times. It was a request he repeated often with us female flight attendants. It wasn't sex, he said, just sitting. One day when he was deadheading back to L.A., I finally had the opportunity to pay him back. He was seated alone in the last row, right across from the parents of another captain. As the service ended and everyone settled into the movie, I noticed our glazed captain sound asleep with his head thrown back and mouth open. I slipped off my shoes, hiked up my skirt, and climbed onto his seat.

I had just straddled him and was over my target when I heard a gasp from across the aisle. "Oh my God!" were the next words I heard. Even in the dark, I saw their eyes and mouth open in shock. The parents were awake and couldn't believe what they saw.

Ed chose that very moment to wake up and started to choke and cough. I was frozen in my straddle position until finally one flight attendant came to my rescue and said, "Just a little Heimlich, folks. Everything's under control." I hope someone on board that night believed him.

I was honored to fly with this man up until his last flight with MGM when he turned sixty and hit the FAA's silly and stupid rule to retire these men out of the pilot seat. MGM paid him well for all his hard work and years with them. They said he could continue as a flight engineer. Unfortunately, without seniority. Well, not quite a sit on the face, but damn close, huh, Ed?

He was such a macho stud that not one of us could really keep from fantasizing about him. Finally, in Barcelona, we decided to do something about it. We were lucky to have hotel rooms with little balconies, and mine just happened to be directly across the courtyard from Captain Ed's.

My coworker Claudia was in my room having a drink before a night out, and I convinced her to help make the trip a memorable one for Ed. We stepped out on my balcony, pulled off our tops, and screamed his name. It took a while but he finally heard us. But then so, too, had the other guests on his side of the building. I didn't need Claudia to translate what those guests were screaming. Old Ed tried to get a picture, but it didn't turn out.

He hounded us to please show those babies off again. It drove him mad. Finally, on his last flight as a captain, we all accommodated his request. No, not the sit-on-the-face request. We were ferrying an empty plane back to Los Angeles and we all took off our tops and served him his last meal at the controls. That time he did get pictures and wouldn't we just love to get them back? Yes, we would, Ed. Yes, we would.

❀ Captain Foot-in-Mouth ❀

You know who you are—the Mel Torme look-alike pilot who always wore cowboy boots and lots of Indian jewelry. Foot-in-Mouth was eventually labeled Diana Without Tits for his ability to piss off the management. (And just when they thought I was their biggest headache.)

How all of us girls laughed as this guy chased us to our rooms, begging to be let in for "just a minute." He was always on the other side of that peephole with the most pathetic puppy dog look. Sometimes with good reason—such as the flight during which I bit his lip. I warned him not to try to kiss me. But he wouldn't listen . . . well, they never listen. Funnier still, when his wife asked about his swollen lip, he told her the truth, and she didn't believe him. Ah, Foot-in-Mouth, I miss you.

We started out not getting along but soon became drinking buddies and reveled in making sexual harassment a dirty word. We also refused to let management get us down, or cut corners when the safest option was the way to go. We shared the knowledge that MGM thrived on stepping over dollars to pick up pennies and risked lives doing it. Management's ill treatment of this pilot only made him more verbal and outrageous.

While he kept waiting for the higher-ups to give it up and promote him, instead they chose intimidation, threats, and harassment. Like the time he flew basketball's Dream Team into Barcelona for the Olympics. Foot-in-Mouth and his crew went to Ireland for their layover. It was there that he received a fax from management naming certain crew members and warning them about their behavior. Of course, Foot-in-Mouth was on the list.

His response to the scolding was to find the bar where the crew was meeting and go in with a paper bag over his head. His theory was that you can't get into trouble if you're in disguise. Good concept, wrong country.

Walking into a bar in Ireland with a bag covering one's head and holes cut out for eyes wasn't the smartest move. The Irish patrons missed the humor, and who could blame them, since they all thought they were under attack. Amazing how he saved his ass and probably his life by quickly coming up with the most ridiculous story about a new miracle cure for hiccups.

After Foot-in-Mouth, they broke the mold.

❀ My Son, Eric ❀

I saved the best for last. My special friend, Eric. I called him my son, because that's really how I saw him. But more than that, Eric was my partner in crime. Finding and getting into trouble on the streets of New York. Together in the bars till sunrise. A witness to my in-flight escapades. Always there for my trials and tribulations. A faithful son who called every day. How he put up with me sometimes I'll never know.

There was one morning when we stumbled out of New York's Emerald Inn and watched two men fighting at the Columbus restaurant. One was inside sitting at a table in front of the glass window to the street. The other brave and tough New Yorker was on the street facing his opponent through the glass. Ah, these macho New York men. They were challenging and taunting one another. Anywhere else you would assume there would be punches thrown.

I found this scene incredibly amusing because all they did was scream the same thing over and over again at each other.

"Fuck you."

"Fuck you."

They answered each other.

"I'll fuck you in the ass," the one shouted.

The other responded, "No, I'll fuck *you* in the ass."

I couldn't stand it another moment and had to get into the act myself. I threw Eric at them and yelled, "Wait, fuck him in the ass. He likes that shit."

There was that split second when we thought we would both be killed, but then remember, this was New York. The two machos just shouted back at us in unison, "Fuck you." Ah, experiencing the Big Apple with your son.

And I can't help but mention the time I was given a new little toy with which to play. It was a tiny recorder with very loud messages that belted out expressions like "You're an asshole," "You're a cock-sucker," "Eat shit."

Someone from MTV had given it to me on a flight, and all the way between New York and L.A., I kept that little toy in my pocket—only to set it off at the perfect moment. It was loud enough to be heard, but hidden enough to drive the passengers crazy trying to figure out who was saying all those things.

Well, after Eric and I left a bar for our walk back to the hotel, I started up again with my toy. Of course, I waited for the most appropriate times to press that button. As we walked past a fruit stand where a man was watering down the sidewalk (is that all they do in N.Y.?), I pressed the button, and much to Eric's chagrin out from nowhere came the line, "You're an asshole, eat shit, you cocksucker."

It was a male voice and Eric was right there, so who knew the grocer would be so sensitive? After he yelled obscenities at Eric, the man hosed him down completely. Poor guy was sopping wet, yet I couldn't stop myself. As we came to another street corner and waited for the light to change, a cop car pulled up. Eric looked at me with pleading eyes. I smiled back and then out it came: "You're a cocksucker."

I quickly pointed to the high-rise across the street and yelled back, "So are you."

The cops looked up at the building and he was off the hook. Pale for wear, but off the hook. I'm sorry, son, I just couldn't stop myself. How do I explain it? When you get to be my age, you just don't want to look back and ask, "Why didn't I?" So I do it and now I look back and ask, "Why did I?" I guess the answer has to be: " 'Cause I wanted to."

Of course, Eric was not so easy having around either. He would love to run into the terminal or to the back of the plane toward me. He would slide down on his back under my skirt and yell, "Italian food. Oh, my God, look at the sauce." Or the time he dragged me into a bar filled with lesbians, and I had to dance with them. He just stood back and laughed. Or the time he introduced me to Channel 35 in New York. The porn commercials. My glimpse at the seedy side of TV. The woman with the enormous breasts that came down to her knees. She would twirl them, then tuck them under her arm and still be able to twirl them. He would call my room and wake me every time she was on.

I did, however, find moments to retaliate, and as often as possible. I still remember the flight when Eric was working the galley and had this enormous gas attack. Poor guy. He tried holding it in, but just as he squatted down to remove a carrier from underneath the microwave, venting occurred in a major way. I noticed him acting rather strangely back there and knew exactly what had happened when I saw him close the curtains in a valiant effort to contain the stench.

It was my cue and I took it. Flinging the curtains open, I screamed much too loudly, "Whoa . . . my God!" Pinching my nose for the entire cabin to see, I flung closed the curtains and stomped back through the cabin, waving my hand as I went to keep the air moving. Eric was so humiliated that he stayed crouched under that microwave for the longest time. Finally, as he moved to stand erect, I got the urge to humiliate once more. Now totally unable to control myself, I picked up the intercom and asked the cockpit to ventilate the cabin. All right, I showed no mercy. But then neither did he.

Whenever the crew would launch into a discussion of the latest Rush Limbaugh show, Eric and I would chat about Howard Stern. (Eric brought such culture into my dull life. Thanks—I think.) He was also the only flight attendant to come hold my hand when I had my hysterectomy. We even had a funeral for my lost womb. He invited friends to come since his mom couldn't anymore. Now that was a bit tacky, not to mention cruel. I think you finally paid me back. But, you're still the best son a mom could have.

4 THE ACTORS

We all recognize their faces. They are famous . . . no, they are *notorious*. These actors with the flashy smiles and occasional sneers. Some are arrogant, some are sweet, all are rich and spoiled. And being on board MGM Grand was not about to change their demeanor. If anything, they felt at home and had the opportunity to relax. Did I say relax? Make that *unfold,* so that every weakness, lust, and insecurity went from secret to exposed in the course of a four-hour flight. Some celebrity passengers, however, did relax and did treat the crew as fellow human beings. Those are memories I treasure.

For many celebrities, though, we were fans, slaves, sex objects . . . and not in that order. And all too often, we were on the receiving end of vented hostility, serving as whipping posts on which the rich, and often unwashed, took out their frustrations. I may never watch another movie—or perhaps I'll watch only a few, with a very select cast, over and over again.

❀ Danny Aiello ❀

Danny Aiello (*Moonstruck*) was always wonderful to have aboard. He's of the old school—a family man, a gentleman, and an Italian who can actually speak the language. On one flight, I was leaning over, practicing flirting in a foreign tongue, when one of the new idiot flight attendants walked by and slapped me on the ass with a silver tray. I ignored him and continued talking until Mr. Aiello interrupted me.

"Wait, did that guy touch you?" he asked.

Not thinking anything of it, I responded, "No, not really."

I started to continue our conversation, but he was still concerned. "I think that guy touched you. I'll punch that son of a bitch out for you. How disrespectful."

I literally had to calm him and hold him down. I know for a fact that my Italian knight would have really done it, socked the kid on the jaw right before he shit in his pants and apologized. Chivalry lived, at least for a moment.

❀ Loni Anderson and Joan Van Ark ❀

These two lovely ladies know how to utilize their time on a four-hour flight. Forget the stimulating conversation around you, ignore the pampering by the crew, turn a blind eye to the view at 35,000 feet. Instead, perfect that glamorous image. Joan applied makeup coast to coast. Loni powdered cleavage from East to West. Well, she *is* stacked.

❀ Lauren Bacall ❀

Not to worry if the younger flight attendants didn't know who she was, she would make sure they found out. It was common to hear, "Do you know who I am? I am Lauren Bacall. THE Lauren Bacall. I was married to Humphrey Bogart. THE Humphrey Bogart." Like any of those young girls knew Bogart either.

Yes, you're right. I could have been nice and prepared the newer girls, but I didn't want to deprive them or our other passengers of an opportunity to see Ms. Bacall at her best and true self. She would always call ahead to make sure we had her fresh veggies from L.A.'s Farmers' Market. The only ones she would allow to be stir-fried for her on board. Of course your veggies were fresh from the Market, Ms. Bacall. Would we ever dream of serving anything else? Well, yes, but only every time.

Apparently caviar was somehow also included on her list of low-cal and healthy allowable cuisine, because if she didn't get three times the amount that everyone else received, heads would roll—and sometimes did.

❀ Billy Baldwin ❀

Or should I say Big Billy Baldwin. Now, this is one well-developed man. How would I know, you ask?

Unfortunately, not the way I would have liked. As it so happens, Billy was interested in one of our more sought-after flight attendants, who eventually succumbed to his charms (like in five minutes). Phone numbers were exchanged on the flight into L.A. and Ms. Cute-as-a-Button was invited by Mr. Baldwin to meet him to attend a birthday party for Martin Short in a Santa Monica eatery.

They had cocktails and conversation, plus a few bites of dinner in between. It was a pleasant evening, and he definitely kept her amused. After all was said and eaten, he came up with the concept of a walk on the beach— but first he wanted to get a sweater from his suite at the Loews Santa Monica Beach Hotel just down the street.

As it turned out, he didn't need his sweater, or any other bits of clothing, for they never made it out of the room that night. And to hear our girl tell it the next day, he was *quite* a surprise in bed. She rated him an 8—unusual for actors since they're so into themselves. When asked why an 8, her response was she was comparing him to Sean Penn, who she felt was a 9+. The girl knows her rulers.

❀ Warren Beatty ❀

He lived up to his terrible reputation with the women. On one particular flight, he couldn't take his eyes off of *Entertainment Tonight*'s Mary Hart. Instead of approaching her directly, he asked a flight attendant to make Mary a hot fudge sundae, and deliver it along with a message.

"Tell her it's from me and I would love to lick it off her body."

She got the sundae and message and sent one back all her own. "Tell him that I am not interested and very happy without him."

Unfazed, Warren continued sending notes to this classy lady, begging her to go out to dinner with him. She stood her ground, as we hoped she would, exiting the plane and stepping into her waiting limo as soon as we touched down in L.A. As for Warren, another flight attendant informed him that his car was late, and as we drove off, Warren was the only passenger left waiting. What a sight. This amorous man alone in the dark, in a gentle rain, not a gal anywhere to be seen.

❀ Candice Bergen ❀

Candice Bergen and her daughter flew several times with Eric, always occupying the same stateroom. He gave the young girl the wings from his uniform, hoping for tickets to a *Murphy Brown* show. What he got was a sweet thank-you. He's still waiting for front-row seats.

❀ Linda Blair ❀

We all adored this actress from *Exorcist* fame and loved having her on our flights. So, too, did singer Freddie

Jackson, whose own head spun around whenever they happened to be aboard the same flight. He kept her enchanted in conversation for the entire four hours of the flight. I even took pictures and sent them copies, hoping to play matchmaker. Freddie returned the favor with an autographed photo, CDs, and his phone number. Linda did not.

❀ Lloyd Bridges ❀

The Bridges family were very familiar faces to us. On rare occasions they would all be together, but more typically it was just Lloyd and his wife, Dorothy. This family had some hardy drinkers, but old Dorothy was the serious one. It was apparent that she was really into it, much to the family's dismay. On one flight, Dad asked me to show him to the restroom and I assumed he had either forgotten his way or was feeling the effects of the alcohol. He was such a sweet, smiling, pleasant man, and I was happy to oblige him, or at least I was until we got to our destination. I opened the lav door for him and with the biggest smile he asked, "Would you care to join me?" Funny thing about that lav. It had a way of making married men forget they had wives.

❀ Downtown Julie Brown ❀

Get down with yourself, girl. What lucky, handsome pilot had a private showing of lingerie by this young lovely in the back of our plush 727?

❀ Gary Busey ❀

A sobering thought: He was on his best behavior with my girlfriend. Maybe it was because he was still recovering from his terrible motorcycle accident. He spoke about how touched he had been by the concern shown by the industry and fans. Off to his house she went to join his other guests. They talked and drank beer as he sang and played his guitar. Later, Sambuca and bed. He just slept. I guess he was sore and tired. No drugs or maybe too many? Since my girlfriend knew CPR, I was surprised she didn't jump-start that man.

When I had Busey on my flights, we would flirt and I'd fantasize, but I'd also wonder what the hell I was really crazy about. On the one hand, he needed his teeth fixed. On the other, it was a great smile. He wasn't handsome, but there was that wild look. I would picture him on his motorcycle and pray that if I were reincarnated I could come back as that seat. I wouldn't let him fall off. Ever.

❀ Red Buttons ❀

Another old-timer and frequent flyer was Red Buttons. We got along famously. He was such a flirt. I never really knew if he wanted more. I never really *wanted* to know if he wanted more.

❀ David Caruso ❀

I had no idea who this cute redhead was when he was on my flight. The only thing I knew was that he was Italian and sexy. A lethal combination.

He was in one of the staterooms with a friend, drinking and flirting. They obviously had had a good start on their liquor before boarding and were ready to party. They were also into the mood for photos, it seemed, for when I dropped by to see if anything needed refreshing, I found myself in David's lap, his arm around me, posing for a snapshot. As the camera flashed, his hand moved higher, finally resting in a vise grip on my left tit.

I don't know which I did first—smacked him or jumped up. He apologized, of course, promising not to show the picture around and to keep his hands to himself in the future. His apology did not keep him from asking for my New York hotel number. It seemed that he liked what he felt and wanted more.

As attractive as I found him, I turned him down. With the alcohol he had consumed, he couldn't remain conscious much longer in any case. Having lived with an alcoholic, I was not eager to spend any time with another.

❀ Cher ❀

Just call her Miss Bitch. When MGM Grand added larger DC-8 aircraft to its fleet and didn't bother to tell anyone but the crew, the reaction ranged from disappointment to hostility. In Cher's case, she felt obliged to vocalize her disappointment, punishing the crew and those around her as she did. Eric was the purser on Cher's first MGM DC-8 flight, and (being a former fan) he swears he doted on her throughout the flight. She was in a stateroom with her sister, Georganne, and Georganne's gorgeous boyfriend. As the saying goes, "Misery loves company," and Cher gave the line new meaning. Yes, Miss Bitch, we remember you still.

❀ Glenn Close ❀

Weather delays and New York go hand in hand. However, Glenn Close felt that the airline and flight crew not only were responsible for the delays but also had the clout to inform traffic control, "We're coming in because Glenn Close says so." I only wish I were exaggerating. Trust me when I say that we were used to the normal bitching, moaning, and whining from our passengers. Glenn Close cranked up the word *scream* to a new level. She not only raised holy hell but stomped her feet in full-blown tantrums as well. And to think she looks so classy on the screen.

❀ Joan Collins ❀

On her first flight with us, the flight attendants were terrified of this woman. Perhaps we believed her advance publicity since we all presumed she would be demanding and difficult to please. I was nominated, as usual, to test the waters.

I took care of Joan in her private stateroom and found her absolutely charming. She carried on a great conversation with me and wasn't the least condescending. In fact, most of her flight time was spent either resting or working on her makeup and adjusting her wig.

The big test came when I discovered that one of my acrylic nails had broken off, and I couldn't find it. With a meek smile, I suggested she check her lunch. This pro didn't even bat an eye as she did just that. (We never did find it.) As for Joan, she seemed more concerned with the fact that I had broken a nail. Lady, you passed my test with flying colors.

❀ Bill Cosby ❀

The Jell-O pitchman and comedy giant was always a welcome passenger on our airline. He usually traveled with his wife, yet always had time for everyone around him, particularly the children. As they would come past his seat, he would lean over into the aisle and whisper (loud enough for us all to hear), "Hey, kid. Want some Jell-O pudding? There's always room for Jell-O." He can offer some to me anytime.

❀ Macaulay Culkin and Family ❀

The *Home Alone* should-a-beens, those Culkin kids, brought terror to the flight attendants even before they boarded the plane. Just having their names on the passenger list was enough to set us off. Mom would sit up front and spend her flight getting drunk and then proceed to hit on the abundant supply of powerful men. All the while, the kids, except for Macaulay, would be seated in the rear of the plane, about as far away from her as they could get without being left in L.A. The children had well-deserved reputations as monsters, making the crews and passengers crazy with their antics. Lots of food, lots of fights, lots of cleanup.

❀ Bette Davis ❀

The great Bette was always assisted onto the plane and never failed to make mention of our snappy flight attendant uniform tuxedos. She chain-smoked, weighed less than ninety pounds, and refused to drink her Ensure. She also insisted on tipping the flight attendants. Smile.

On one occasion, Bette set off the alarm while passing through security. She was turned back and asked to walk through again. Again the alarm sounded, and with it, those famous eyes of hers widened in displeasure. Faster than they've ever moved before, the security team whipped out their handwand and did a quick pass as Bette, her cane waving, stomped away without ever looking back. How could you not love this old gal?

❀ Robert DeNiro ❀

Robert DeNiro is one tough guy. And a man who loves women of color. It was typical for him to pursue the black flight attendants with vigor, sending dozens of roses to their hotel rooms in New York, or picking them up by limo for a little fun in the city.

Now, I wouldn't have minded such hand-holding after my long days of feeding and watering the elite, but he only had eyes for others. Those that he liked were extravagantly rewarded. One attendant returned from an evening with Bobby carrying a large garment bag. Inside was an awesome, full-length mink coat. We oohed and aahed as she displayed her prize but later gathered in the back of the plane for the real laughs. This particular flight attendant's husband had appeared on a talk show about interracial marriage. He had raved about the strength of their union. He was happy to be married to a flight attendant, he said. One only wonders what story she came up with to explain the mink showing up in her baggage. Would he believe that it came from our lost-and-found department, or perhaps we were just the best tipped in the industry?

DeNiro, for his part, was always rather close-lipped about his liaisons. Given his full-time girlfriends and sometime wives, he had to be. One evening, while he sat waiting to board in our lounge in New York with then-girlfriend Toukie Smith, he got the news that his flight to L.A. was to be delayed for several hours. The crew ended up serving the passengers caviar, appetizers, and part of their in-flight meal to help settle the restless. DeNiro and Smith consumed every bite they could, plus a tankful of vodka, Scotch, and tequila, before bailing on the flight and slipping off into the night.

❀ Danny DeVito and Rhea Perlman ❀

Danny DeVito was never a problem as long as he traveled alone. One evening in the Grand Lounge at JFK Airport in New York, while we all waited out yet another long weather delay, I was pointed out to DeVito as MGM Grand's resident comic, and he was pushed in my direction. This short-statured man came up behind me and tapped me on the shoulder. As I whipped around, given the difference in our heights, he got a bust in his mouth. There was a great deal of laughter as we both turned shades of pink.

What else could I do? I looked at him and said, "Don't even try to speak with your mouth full." Things in the room lightened up considerably after that.

When he didn't travel solo, things were quite different. Some flight attendants complained that his wife, actress Rhea Perlman, was not the most pleasant to have on board. For such a short woman, they felt she still managed to look down on the help. When the rest of the family traveled with them, we had even more of a problem. The general complaint from the crews was that they brought their own food on board and really made themselves at home in the stateroom. The cleaning crew would always be amazed at how much damage this one family accomplished in such a short period of time, and wondered if they had brought their trash from home with them, as well.

❀ Patty Duke ❀

Patty Duke was a smoker, and she somehow felt that we would bend the FAA nonsmoking rules just for her. Some flight attendants actually obliged her and demonstrated how to sneak cigs—the theory being that at least that way we would know when, where, and who. I would dump her in the lav with a container of water and a cigarette. And then go in immediately after she vacated to check for burning embers. It's the unknown that will get you.

❀ Gordon Elliott ❀

Gordon Elliott, the talk show host, flew once in a stateroom with his girlfriend. Not atypically, they had a good time, got drunk, and ended up removing articles of clothing. Being the modest type particularly where fat men are concerned, I slid their curtains closed. I'm not certain if they joined the Mile High

Club during the flight, but I do know that as we were landing, Gordon left his mark by throwing up all over the stateroom. Class shows.

⊛ Farrah Fawcett ⊛

If Cher hadn't already owned the title, Farrah Fawcett would have been dubbed Miss Bitch. She was one of the most spoiled and uncontrolled passengers, particularly after a few drinks. Not just any drink, of course. Only certain brands of liquor were good enough for Miss Mouth-With-Ten-Too-Many-Teeth.

On one flight in which Farrah was traveling with Alana Hamilton and Jerry Hall, one of the more ingenious among us decided to show her exactly who was *really* in charge on board by offering to concoct her a "special" drink. It consisted of Bailey's, vodka, Kahlua, milk, and crushed ice. While it wasn't an easy sell, finally Miss I-Know-What-I-Like agreed to taste the special elixir.

A moment later the special brew was ready for delivery with an added new ingredient courtesy of two of our more offended troop: the best and biggest wads of spit they could produce. After the lovely Miss Fawcett tasted the drink, her taste buds apparently jumped for joy. Only seconds later she was back in the galley totally excited. "I want only you to make our drinks from now on," announced the luscious one. "And make them *exactly* the same." Well, she asked for it.

Who were we to deny a star? The hardest thing was keeping a straight face. Tip: Never piss off the kitchen help until the end of the flight.

❀ Harrison Ford ❀

Nice guy Harrison Ford was on board with his family one day, when it was discovered that the proud new parents had forgotten to bring an extra outfit for their baby. And, as luck would have it, the little one wiped out what he was wearing.

"No biggie," said one of our own. "I'll just dry it for you in the microwave." Good idea; wrong clock. As the tiny outfit sat in the micro cooking, it progressed from wet, to damp, to dry, to hot, to burning within a matter of seconds.

Harrison Ford was very understanding, saying, "We're just going straight to the limo." I wonder if he felt the same when they were surprised by the paparazzi upon arrival, anxious to snap everything including baby's bottom. Ah, sweet success.

❀ Larry Fortensky ❀

MGM Grand was the charter of choice when Elizabeth Taylor volunteered to help out Michael Jackson in his hour of need. Elizabeth, along with then-hubby Larry Fortensky, flew to London, then on to Ireland and Geneva. When asked midway what he thought of the

Hollywood scene, Fortensky was heard to utter: "I think it stinks. All these people I don't know keep kissing me at these stupid functions. I can't stand it. I just give them my hand." But then, he does work with his hands now, doesn't he?

❀ Jodie Foster ❀

Jodie Foster boarded alone. So, too, did Kelly McGillis. Despite the fact that they were seated rows apart, they seemed to be drawn toward one another. What followed next was not unlike a mating dance. One at a time, they ever so casually made it to the bar after the food service was finished and started with light banter. Soon they were into deep conversation.

While the rest of the passengers were distracted and watching the movie, the crew saw Jodie and Kelly move discreetly into Jodie's stateroom. How deep (in conversation) did they get in that dark and private stateroom? No one knew, the crew opting to remain in the dark as well.

❀ Michael J. Fox, Dana Carvey, Connie Chung ❀

There they were on the same flight—Connie Chung in her usual place up front; Michael J. Fox and Dana Carvey next to one another, midcabin. We should have guessed that something would happen. It seemed to be in the air—right along with the rest of us.

Connie Chung ranked as one of my favorite passengers and I looked forward to seeing her once or twice a week. It was an important part of our job to know our passengers' likes and dislikes. While no reciprocation was required or expected, this intelligent, charming, and kind lady had the class to remember not only my name but also everything I had ever discussed with her. She would amaze me when she'd comment on my latest change in hair color and ask about my kids—by name. (Thank you, Connie. The kids are fine.)

Michael J. Fox was definitely one of our frequent travelers. In the early and less restrictive MGM Grand days, he was able to bring his dog on board and have him seated at his feet. The girls all wanted to eat him up (Michael, not the dog).

On this particular flight all three came on cheerful, as usual, but Michael and Dana were definitely in the mood to party. While the boys kept us busy pouring the booze, Michael confided to me that he had always thought Connie was sexy (and I'm sure he meant to add intelligent). On and on he went for the next couple of hours, Connie this and Connie that.

Like a schoolboy with a crush on his teacher, Michael finally got up the nerve to get up and go talk to her. (All right, I pushed him into it. So what? I started the boys out with mimosas, followed by beer, then wine with brunch. I then polished them off after brunch with Kahlua, vodka, and Bailey's. They were going to need a stomach pump after this flight or at least one hell of a nap. But one way or another Michael was going to speak to Connie.)

When the conversation finally occurred, it was short, sweet, and apparently politely negative, for Michael returned to his seat somewhat dejected. Dana, less affected by the booze but having one hell of a good time, kept Michael and everyone else in stitches. With his head reeling, poor Michael was easy prey as Dana egged him into focusing his attention on a Demi Moore look-alike flight attendant.

It was always clear that Michael was very much in love with his wife, actress Tracy Pollan. He never had a wandering eye or flirted when on board. But it was different this day, thanks to Dana's influence and the booze.

The flight was a typical "run your ass off" one, and it was a challenge to keep up with the passenger demands—not to mention these two drunk babies. To keep myself going, I sipped water and sneaked a snack. I had just popped a handful of nuts into my mouth when the call button rang down the aisle. As I charged past Michael he grabbed my arm and uttered those words any girl loves to hear: "You are so hot." He then proceeded to pull me onto his little lap.

The next thing I knew his tongue was in my mouth. Swell, me with a mouthful of nuts and Fox. What a disgrace to the flight attendant community. It should have been a mouthful of Fox's nuts. (Oh, sorry about the typo. Of course I meant a mouthful of Fox.) A professional flight attendant never works with her mouth full.

Dana seemed to take a certain pride in having moved Michael's image from innocent boy to slurring, flirting, grabbing man. As more passengers began to see what happened, Michael's embarrassment grew and grew. As word spread throughout the plane, even dear Connie wanted to know if everything was all right.

Emerging to prying eyes, I moved down the aisle to reassure Connie that everyone was fine. I told her that Michael was just trying to get to her through me. At the other end of the plane, Michael's call button rang.

"Please, promise you won't say a word, especially to my wife when she's traveling with me," he begged. I assured him I would never say a word. I waited just long enough for a relieved look to cross his face before adding, "I'll let the *National Enquirer* tell her." Poor baby looked so devastated, I couldn't keep him in pain a second longer. "Lighten up, kid," I added with a wink.

That would have been the end of the story, if Michael hadn't had to upchuck into one barf bag after another as the plane was making its final descent into L.A. Dana, of course, used the moment for more comedy material. Barf bags make such wonderful props.

Once on the ground, Michael crawled off the aircraft only to be greeted by the blazing Los Angeles sun and a pool of paparazzi. Boy, did they miss a story.

❀ *Zsa Zsa Gabor* ❀

It was just after the much-publicized slapping incident with the Beverly Hills cop that Zsa Zsa Gabor flew to New York to do the *Geraldo Rivera* talk show. It was the morning flight, and it was filled with our usual assortment of celebrities—none of whom seemed any too anxious to acknowledge poor Zsa Zsa in her time of need.

In an effort to appear nonplussed, she kept asking various flight attendants to pass notes to other passengers for her. As it turned out, none came to her rescue. Despite being ostracized, everything would have been fine if she had only kept her mouth shut. Unfortunately, she didn't seem able to remain silent.

"Dahling, is there something wrong with this airline?" she asked Eric as she was deplaning. "Are you going bankrupt? There wasn't any caviar." After he explained as quietly as he could that caviar wasn't served on morning flights, she still felt it necessary to have the last word. "Good, because I must have my caviar," she said.

It was more than a passenger standing behind her could handle. To the laughs of those around him, he said, "Bitch, where you're going, there ain't no caviar."

She turned, and for the briefest moment, I thought she was going to do it. Slap his face. No such luck. It would have made the perfect end to this story. Well, there's always the next time.

❀ Richard Gere ❀

The gay community has discussed this actor's sexuality and interest in gerbils for years. But gerbils had nothing to do with my gay coworker's nervousness while trying to take Gere's dinner order. He thought this hunk was too gorgeous for words and, because of it, was barely able to function around the man. He was so nervous that, try as he might, he couldn't stop tapping his pencil against his clipboard as he was staring down into Gere's mane of beautiful black-gray hair.

Quite suddenly, the pencil flew from his grasp and went sailing in the air, landing right smack in between Gere's legs. While I would have known instantly what to do (well, I *am* Italian), this flight attendant hadn't a clue. After an awkward moment, he asked timidly, "Um, shall I get it?"

Gere, totally enjoying the moment, responded, "If you want it, then you should."

My friend was so flustered, he could only just pick up the pencil and run like hell. I'm just happy we didn't have gerbil on the menu.

❀ Whoopi Goldberg ❀

Whoopi Goldberg was by far the best passenger. She was funny, kind, and always a pleasure to have on board. She was, however, a smoker and would try to sneak those cigs in the lav. She tried to be so cool about lighting up, as if we really didn't know. Honey, we knew. We'd wait for her to come out and say, "Girl, stop blowing the smoke into the toilet bowl. It's a bitch to get the blue out of those dreadlocks." Then we would add: "If you do the safety demo, we'll pull the circuit breaker for you."

Well, like I said, she was a smoker, and it was a four-hour flight. She couldn't pass up such a good bargain. She always did a great demo and made certain every passenger (finally) paid attention. They loved her performance so much, she'd get applause, whistles, and cheers of appreciation. (Our favorite moment was when she got to the "no smoking" part of the routine.) What an actress. What a flight attendant!

❀ Kelsey Grammer ❀

Mail from a fellow flight attendant:

Dear Diana,
I had Kelsey Grammer on last night. He drank the whole bottle of Beefeater gin. He kept telling me how beautiful I was and how he wanted to take me out. He asked me for my phone number, but then couldn't even write it down.

I saw him stumbling and heading for the bathroom, and I got there just in time to catch him falling into the door. He pulled me in there with him, and we both went flying into the toilet. God, what a sight!

He then started hurling. After that, I helped him back up, but he got mad at me when I wouldn't let him stick his tongue into my mouth. He may be a star, but he had just puked, for God's sake, and he thought I'd want his tongue in my mouth. How's that for gratitude! For pulling Kelsey out of the shitter.

He was in the same condition on another flight when the flight attendant went into the stateroom to wake him up from his stupor. He fell on the floor and grabbed her legs and begged for a date while crying out his love for her.

❀ Arsenio Hall ❀

While white guys Robert DeNiro and *Rocky*'s Burt Young loved our black flight attendants, our African-American star passengers seemed to gravitate toward blondes. Among them was Arsenio Hall. Arsenio spotted one of our younger and more naive girls back in the galley and pursued her during the entire flight. He offered her tickets to his then–talk show and backstage passes, and when he saw her arrive on the set, he tried once more to make his move. Perhaps his good friend Magic Johnson had clued him in as to how easy we were on MGM. As it turned out, this young thing was far from easy, having just become engaged to her strapping beau. In any case, she swears that nothing happened, and I believe her. Just because Arsenio was cute, and rich, and reported to be well hung . . . nah, nothing happened.

❀ Tom Hanks ❀

The first time Tom Hanks came on board, he was on his way to New York to publicize his new film *Big*. The flight was full, and instead of a table, Eric had to strap on a tray for him. It was so comical, like a man in a high chair. Tom and his wife, actress Rita Wilson, prove that fame and fortune don't automatically translate into boring and conceited. They were neither. Rather, they were obviously in love—with each other and life. A standing ovation for this pair.

❀ Robert Hays ❀

There he was, running down the jetway, panting, struggling not to miss the plane. Robert Hays of *Airplane!* fame barely made it. The door was just about shut when I spied him out of the corner of my eye.

"No, no!" I screamed as he tried to step on board. You're not getting on *this* plane." He screeched to a halt and stared at me, a curious, nonbelieving kind of "huh?" stare. "The cockpit is having fish for dinner, and you're afraid to fly. Sorry, we can't take any chances!"

Finally, he got the point that I was kidding, and to my relief replied, "It's okay. I got help. I'm cured. I can do this, really." Fortunately, he never had to re-create his *Airplane!* movie role on one of our flights.

❀ Charlton Heston ❀

I don't know where the connection came from, but Charlton Heston seemed to be the airline's unofficial ambassador or spokesman. He was the guest of honor for our inaugural flight and traveled with us often. The first time I watched him board our plane, I couldn't get out of my mind the picture of him parting the Red Sea. It was a vision that soon faded, however.

He had just eaten and dozed off when it hit. Charlton Heston cut the cheese. It was hard to remember that this man was a legend while you were gagging for fresh air. We thought we were dying and most of the passengers were complaining.

I finally called the cockpit and asked for help. I never thought this Catholic girl would have to say that Moses broke wind and was killing us. If something didn't happen and happen quick, I thought we would have to make an emergency landing. One of the passengers called me over and asked if maybe Mr. Heston needed a doctor. I sniffed the air and said, "More like a priest."

❀ Dennis Hopper ❀

Flight attendant tip: When doing the safety demo for Dennis Hopper, you will be required to repeat the part about breathing normally with an oxygen mask over your nose and mouth. Repeat over—and slowly. He liked to remind me that he was quite experienced with breathing normally while his nose and mouth were covered. I would have been only too happy to verify that fact using my own personal body parts as props, but he never asked me.

Ironically, the first time I met Dennis, I was dead-heading out of uniform on MGM back to Los Angeles. I was seated next to him for lunch. We struck up a conversation and eventually the subject came around to my occupation. I told him that I was in casting. His interest intensified immediately and he asked about the project I was currently working on.

"Nothing special," I answered, my face totally serious. "Just a porno." At that point, *nothing* could have gotten him out of his seat. Yes, I eventually confessed that I was making a joke, but not before I worked that man into a frenzy.

❀ Whitney Houston ❀

On one flight, Whitney was traveling with a female companion. They were both in a stateroom lying down—next to each other. Could those rumors be true?

On the next flight, she was with her husband, Bobby Brown. While she was sitting up front, he was in the back of the plane visiting and flirting with the flight attendants. Yes, he asked for phone numbers; yes, he got them.

Can this woman ever leave home with fewer than

a hundred suitcases? She flew MGM Grand because the other airlines would charge for the overage. We never did. Clever Whitney.

❀ Anjelica Huston ❀

Anjelica Huston happened to be on board with her boyfriend (now husband), Robert Graham, when we had to make an emergency landing in Denver. It had been a routine flight to Los Angeles until we got word from the cockpit to collect the oxygen bottles from various locations throughout the plane. We had no sooner announced to the passengers that we needed to make an unscheduled stop in Denver than we were smacked with panic from the Huston-Graham camp.

They were nervous flyers to begin with and wanted to get off the plane as soon as the wheels hit the tarmac. Unfortunately, we couldn't get an immediate gate clearance, and it was some time before one was assigned. In an effort to calm shattered nerves, Eric took Anjelica to the back of the plane for a cigarette. Her hand was shaking as she vainly tried to light up.

When we finally found an empty gate, Anjelica and Robert were the first off the aircraft and the only ones who decided against coming back on board. For all I know, they're still in Denver.

❀ Raul Julia ❀

The late Raul Julia was handsome, sexy, and a gentleman. On one flight he asked me for assistance. His back suspenders had come loose. Could I help him, please? Could I? Could I ever. So close. So tight.

Yeah, I helped him. I was a little lady. I behaved. Well, sort of. I decided his shirt tail needed to be tucked in and did it. He glanced over his shoulder and in his wonderful, sexy Latin voice said, "Thank you, you are so kind."

I melted immediately and responded softly, "You're welcome. Call me if you spill anything."

❀ Mark and Brian ❀

Popular L.A. deejays Mark and Brian took it upon themselves (with a little help from the United Service Organizations and MGM) to bring holiday greetings to our troops in Saudi Arabia during Operation Desert Storm. The "Mark and Brian Desert Cheer" flight was sponsored by MGM, with the boys planning to broadcast from a Saudi base after delivering messages from home.

Our DC-8 was loaded with goodies donated by our regular passengers: NBA teams, Mrs. Fields cookies, Bijan, Tova, Nike—over fifteen tons of gifts in all. Unfortunately, the one thing that the troops really wanted, and that we couldn't supply due to Saudi customs, was beer.

Beer or no beer, the flight was set. The crew was being selected and assigned on a strictly volunteer basis. Only four flight attendants could go. Since I had seniority, the flight was offered to me, and I jumped at the chance. Soon my phone was ringing nonstop with offers of bribes from junior flight attendants. They were assisted by the in-flight supervisors who barraged my answering machine with warnings of how exhausting the trip would be. They had a point. The flight took twenty to twenty-five hours each way, with nonstop service, no crew relief, and on and on. Still, there was no way I was going to give it up and I'm glad I didn't.

There are always glitches, even in the best of plans, and we hit a big one. Washington refused to give clearance for the deejays to get off the plane in Dhahran. The base commanding officer was concerned with Mark and Brian's reputation and apparently thought these guys would bad-mouth the impending war and lower morale. We were actually in the air before we even got authority to land. We stopped in Scotland for fuel and received the good news there.

There were more problems soon after, however. While flying over Austria, of all places, we were informed that if we didn't make a 180° turn immediately and leave Austrian airspace, the Austrian Air Force would do it for us. Our pilots didn't have to be asked twice. We turned tail and ended up over the Adriatic Sea.

When we finally arrived at our destination, we flung open the airplane door and stood there with big smiles, expecting a cheering group of grateful servicemen and -women. What we got were looks of puzzlement. No one had bothered to inform the troops that we were coming, or who the hell we were. We just started yelling at them and throwing T-shirts and hats. The first to pay any attention to us were three gorgeous and sexy paratroopers, in their jumpsuits, no less. Where did we get that newfound energy?

My initial conversation with one of these gorgeous men went along these lines: One of them said, "Wow, you smell great. It's been months since I smelled perfume. Could I just sniff your neck?"

Of course, I said yes. I was feeling *very* patriotic. After a quick sniff, my paratrooper added: "It's been months since I kissed or held a woman." Still eager to support our troops, I obliged with a quick kiss. Then I heard, "I haven't *had* a woman in months." Too cute.

At that moment, I realized my patriotism only ran so deep and responded: "Listen, handsome, don't push your luck. You got a T-shirt, hat, sniff, and kiss. There is no way you're getting laid, too." After all, I had just flown for twenty-some hours and for free, no less. One of the other troopers, however, made out far better and managed to get very friendly with one of the other female flight attendants—Kujo, of all people. I heard that they even got together months later when he returned to the States.

After leaving the plane, we started our own public relations program. They escorted us around the base and then decided to take us on a quick tour outside the base. I don't think Saudi Arabia was quite ready for four women strolling the streets with makeup, short skirts, and attitude. It made for plenty of looks.

Always one to push the envelope, I decided to give them a *real* show. Telling our escorts to "gather around and stay close," I proceeded to light a cigarette.

In return for our season's greetings and good cheer, we were given some local food to take home. It turned out to be the last thing we needed for our return flight. Pattee, my flying partner, spent the entire flight home alternating between hugging the toilet and sitting on it.

The trip back had a different mood. The homesick troops took a toll on the deejays. Mark and Brian were emotionally drained by their encounter with the boys they had taped. Everyone, including these two wild and crazy deejays, had tear-filled eyes, and it was a quiet flight. No one wanted to leave the troops behind. Thank God they eventually made it home.

❀ Bette Midler ❀

The biggest surprise was how unfriendly, unfunny, and surly Bette Midler could be. We all considered it a blessing when she didn't acknowledge us. On one particular flight, she was accompanied by her husband

and new baby, and they settled into a stateroom. Right across the hall, Steven Seagal, his then-wife, Kelly LeBrock, and their baby were getting comfortable.

As the flight progressed, the toddlers became restless, and both sets of parents decided to let their respective little tykes play together in the aisle. Now that was a sight. The beautiful Seagal child and the, well—to be kind, it was a contrast. Yeah, that's what it was, a contrast.

❀ Eddie Murphy ❀

Eddie always traveled with his abundant entourage. He quickly earned the reputation of being difficult and a snob. Fortunately, his attitude mellowed when he fell in love and became a father. Soon after, he met my youngest daughter on a flight, and I'll never forget how sweet he was with her. Every time I saw him after that point, he always called me "Heather's mom."

On one particular flight, we happened to be down a crew member, and I warned him in advance that our service might be a little slower than normal. His reaction was to instruct a couple of his guys to get up and give us some help. All our passengers should have been so gracious.

The flight attendant I nicknamed Body Beautiful had a special reason to remember Eddie Murphy. He invited her out to dinner, and they were joined by Mike Tyson. Not a bad reward for scraping someone's plate.

❀ Bill Murray ❀

Just call him Wild Bill. He was so much fun to have on flights. The first time we flew together he was with Dan Akroyd, and the two just couldn't stop gabbing at the bar. I can't remember ever laughing so hard—at least, not while I was fully clothed.

It was Wild Bill who, on another occasion, took it upon himself to lighten the mood while we were stuck in our Grand Lounge in New York waiting for the weather to break. Bill started pushing a cart up and down and serving appetizers. Thank goodness for stars like him.

❀ Leslie Nielsen ❀

Leslie Nielsen was never without his whoopee cushion. He was a walking case of flatulence. You never really saw the cushion, but you could always hear it as he spoke, no matter how serious the conversation. We were always ready when we saw his name on the manifest, stocking his seat with Gas-X, Rolaids, and Alka-Seltzer. You couldn't say we weren't prepared for everything on MGM Grand.

❀ Ryan O'Neal ❀

Ryan enjoyed his free champagne on our flights. I mean, *really* enjoyed it. As the bubbly flowed, so did his mouth. It wasn't unusual for Ryan to get himself completely drunk. And with drunk comes loud.

As the flight made its approach for landing, the lights were dimmed, the music turned off. A quiet time, except on one particular flight. Ryan was disturbing the other passengers with his rantings. When the elderly wife of a producer asked the flight attendant to speak to Ryan about keeping it down a little, and the flight attendant dutifully complied, his response was an eloquent "Fuck 'em. Fuck 'em!" Not quite finished, he turned around to the sweet lady and shouted loudly, "Fuck you." Does this man have even an ounce of talent, because he certainly doesn't have that much class.

❀ Judd Nelson ❀

How do you impress a long-legged, blond MGM flight attendant? If you are Judd Nelson, you invite her to a movie. Oh wait, first you rent out the entire theater so you are completely alone. I don't know about you, but that just might work with me. Seems like some of the Brat Pack grew up.

❀ Edward James Olmos ❀

He came on a flight to New York with the biggest smile and used it to his advantage. With those sexy Latin eyes, he walked up to the flight attendant and asked for a personal tour of the plane. "I'd love to see the galley in the back and I've heard so much about the aft lav." How could anyone have turned down a request like that?

She took him on a tour and pretended she didn't realize he wanted her in the lav with him. They teased each other without ever saying what was on either of their minds.

Chemistry being chemistry, he spent the rest of the flight talking to her before discreetly asking where she was staying in the city. Our girl not-so-discreetly told him. After the meal service, he stood at the bar with the crew and managed to find out more about his chosen target. Little facts. Like the news she couldn't drink champagne without taking off her clothes, and that the most sensitive part of her body were her feet.

That evening in New York he telephoned, saying that he was finished with his business and was on his way to pick her up. She dressed for an evening out on the town. When she opened her door, she was greeted with a bottle of champagne. A man of few words, he scooped her up in his arms and carried her to the bed—popping the cork, so to speak.

He reminded her of his image, well respected in the Hispanic community. He was a little too into his physical image as well, checking himself out in the mirror and admiring his new, sleeker physique. He told her about his last affair, which his wife had discovered. It seemed that wifey got back at him by returning the favor and now things weren't so great at home. And this was going to improve things?

"So please, be discreet," he said. "I know I can trust you." Talk about ego.

The flight attendant was discreet. In the crew van the next morning, however, it was very quiet. To break the silence, someone said, "Hey, guess what actor I saw coming out of one of our hotel rooms last night?" She had our attention. "It was Edward James Olmos."

All heads turned to the guilty flight attendant. From the back of the van, another flight attendant commented, "I thought I heard the *Miami Vice* theme coming from your room."

❀ Sean Penn ❀

This relationship started as a phone friendship because both Sean Penn and the flight attendant had busy schedules that never jibed. After many attempts to rendezvous, the pair linked calendars and appointment books.

They went for pizza and beer in Redondo Beach where, of course, he was recognized and hounded for autographs, then on to his house, which, she said, was comfortable and unpretentious. The pleasant evening was capped off by sex. I had to know . . . I had to ask. . . . Well, how was he?

"Great," she said. "Better than Baldwin." After all, Sean was more than just a one-night stand. They had become friends. I find it best not to say what I think about that statement. Size? Average. Ahh, but he took her to breakfast the next morning. Then he went on his merry way to be with girlfriend (now wife) Robin Wright. Actors.

❀ Anthony Perkins ❀

The late Anthony Perkins loved to play, particularly with Eric and his mouth. Ironically, Eric hadn't met Tony aboard a flight but rather years before when he was a drug courier for his roommate. Eric delivered cocaine to Tony and wife Berrie Berenson at their home in L.A.'s Nichols Canyon. The drug runs had gone on for some time until Eric's roommate got arrested. The roommate went to jail and Eric became a flight attendant. Sometimes life works like that.

The last time Eric saw Berrie was aboard one of our flights to New York. She recognized him from the old days. Eric looked the same. Berrie was nearly unrecognizable, the years of cocaine having taken their toll.

At any rate, Berrie confided to Eric that Tony was quite ill and that he didn't have long to live. I caught a glimpse of him as he met his wife and he did indeed look very frail. He died only days later.

❀ Joe Piscopo ❀

He was a frequent passenger. His "babysitter"/girl-friend normally joined him in the lav. One time, I saw another flight attendant go in after them to clean up.

"Did they leave anything behind?" I asked.

"Just two straws." A health drink?

❀ Dennis Quaid and Meg Ryan ❀

Dennis Quaid and wife Meg Ryan were two of our favorites. Cute, funny, kind, sexy. Who says you can't have it all and more?

❀ Molly Ringwald ❀

What was it with this woman? The former Brat Packer had a problem answering questions. She continually hid her face behind a menu. Shy? Insecure? Or just a real brat?

❀ Julia Roberts ❀

When you are a flight attendant with MGM, what is proper procedure when Julia Roberts and Jason Patric go into the bathroom for a long, long time? Well, this is special. You gather up your coworkers and wait for the couple to emerge. You then congratulate them on joining the Mile High Club and present them with their own set of wings.

On subsequent flights, though, I'd wonder if this woman was ever happy. She would stay in a stateroom with the curtains drawn and cry for five hours nonstop.

❀ Mickey Rourke ❀

Mickey Rourke and girlfriend (now wife) Carré Otis were sloshed and lovey-dovey. Of course they asked, like so many others before them, that the curtains to their stateroom be closed. I only hope they kept their seatbelts fastened low and tight as they were fucking their way into the Mile High Club.

❀ Cybill Shepherd ❀

It didn't take much booze to get this one's tongue wagging about Bruce Willis. The rumors that they hated one another must have been true if her description of Willis is any indication. Words like *jerk, obnoxious, unprofessional,* and *asshole* ring in memory. So tell us, Cybill, what do you *really* think?

❀ Maria Shriver ❀

Not exactly an actor, but a walking endorsement for the power of makeup. Thank God not all women who don't shave their legs are as rude as this one. She would come on board and immediately demand a footstool. Funny, every time we watched this woman walk, we would hum the song "Walk Like a Man."

❀ Richard Simmons ❀

Should Richard Simmons be listed with the actors or the comics? Considering the way he behaved, it's a toss-up. The first time he flew MGM Grand, he was dancing up and down the aisles singing to the passengers. Poor Eric was so frightened he decided to stay hidden in the galley for as long as possible. Unfortunately, as the passengers were deplaning, Simmons walked right up to Eric and said, "Now this one has got to go. He ignored me the whole flight. I'm devastated."

Eric, being the polite son he is, immediately apologized, at which point Simmons slipped him his hotel number and said that he could make it up to him later. Eric was luckier than the purser, who got a wet kiss for *not* ignoring him the whole flight. Luckily, the purser was gay, so he handled it well. Moist towelettes for everyone.

❀ O.J. Simpson ❀

Long before I ever saw O.J. Simpson on one of our flights, I spotted him in the bars and clubs in New York, a typical prowler and player like the rest of the former athletes. I looked forward to meeting him. After all, his old team, the Buffalo Bills, was my favorite, and I remembered him well.

Finally, the moment arrived. He ended up not only on MGM Grand, but in my section. Whoa. Was I in for a disappointment. He instantly gave me the creeps with his two distinct personalities. Alone, he made it clear that I was a woman and "hired help," both obviously low in his estimation. Yet, when he was around his peers or if he was aware another passenger was watching or listening, he became polite and respectful, knowing how to turn on the charm and keep up the persona.

When he flew with Nicole, he was the perfect gentleman. When he flew alone, he was flirting with his favorites—the young blond flight attendants. But even that attraction wasn't consistent. On one occasion, he invited a big-busted Nicole look-alike flight attendant out to party in New York. Unfortunately, the flight attendant started the drugs and drinking before the event. She got to the door and O.J. was happy to see her until he realized she had been drinking.

He got belligerent and nasty and called her a slut and drunken whore. It was the wrong thing to say. She shouted her own obscenities back at him before lifting her blouse to show him what he was missing. O.J. lunged at her, forgetting that this was a girl who knew how to evacuate an entire plane in minutes. She and the flight attendants with her were out of there in less than a New York minute and into a cab.

On another evening after a flight during which he'd been flirting with a particular blond flight attendant, we ran into him at Nell's, a popular hangout in New York. He stood next to us at the bar, but now he snubbed the very same blond flight attendant he had hit on earlier. "Weird" was all she could say. He had invited other girls to meet him at private clubs and then changed his mind and barred their entrance.

My biggest regret is that I won't ever have the opportunity to have this man as a passenger again. I'd dream of encountering him on a flight filled with his peers. I would set the table resplendent with crystal, china, and silver. He would notice something was missing and wave to get my attention.

"Miss, where's my knife?" he would ask. I would pretend not to hear. I'd look confused. He would ask again, raising his voice. "Where is my knife?"

"Ask Kardashian," I would respond, loud enough for all to hear.

A challenge to all flight attendants and food servers. Please do it for me. Skip his knife (and then add a little something extra to his food and beverage).

❀ Suzanne Somers ❀

Suzanne was a sweetheart and always full of advice. Since we both lived with alcoholics, we had lots to discuss. (I wish her Thigh Master had been as helpful to me.)

After our chat I made up a bed for her and her husband, Alan Hamel. I pulled the curtains shut and made sure no one disturbed them. Well, after all, three's company.

❁ Tori Spelling ❁

She was so nervous about flying that for security she would hug her teddy bear during takeoffs and landings. That must be why she had her head in her boyfriend's lap for so long. Turbulence can be so hard on some flyers. Makes you never want to leave your zip code.

❁ The Stallones ❁

No one quite knew how to prepare for Sylvester Stallone's mother, Jacqueline. She was usually outrageous, holding everyone's attention with dish about her family—particularly about Sly's second wife, Brigitte Nielsen. As for Stallone's brother, Frank, he mistakenly thought he was God's special creation and acted like a jerk to me. I took the opportunity to remind him what a Sicilian woman could do to a man. He eventually got the point, but not before engaging in verbal warfare with me for an entire flight.

❀ Meryl Streep ❀

What a gal. Eric was serving Meryl Streep some tortellini appetizer before he had quite mastered the art of French service. There he was straddling her legs, which she had extended over a footstool, juggling serving utensils and slippery noodles. As he lifted the first helping onto her plate, a stray tortellini took flight. We all froze watching this baby sail.

Just as calm as you please, Meryl cupped her hands and caught that tortellini like a shortstop, popping it into her mouth.

"Eric, it was delicious. I'll have more," she said.

Like I said, what a gal.

❀ Elizabeth Taylor ❀

I had been selling AIDS ribbons to the crew to raise money for a memorial fund for a coworker who had recently died of AIDS. Management went out of its way to make certain we all knew that we couldn't wear the ribbons on our uniforms. I, of course, wore mine. I couldn't understand the hypocrisy. MGM had given a $50,000 AIDS donation to Magic Johnson after his announcement. So what were they trying to say?

Ironically soon after, Elizabeth Taylor was brought on the flight in a wheelchair and settled into a stateroom. I had fixed up the bed for her and her adorable dog. She was warm, kind, easy to talk to, and appreciative of everything done for her.

She couldn't help but notice my AIDS ribbon, and after I told her the story (including the part about the corporate attitude), she seemed impressed that I continued to break the rules to pay homage to those who had died from the disease. Innocently (well, maybe not *so* innocently), I asked her what she thought MGM would do if they got a letter from someone of her stature complaining about the ribbon policy, and I left it at that. Within days of that conversation, corporate policy was changed and we were allowed to wear our ribbons. Management even donated enough to our fund for us to meet our goal.

❀ Kathleen Turner ❀

You could actually watch her swell, bloat, and gain weight while she drank. It was always a contest to see how much booze it took to swell her tongue, since she gave new meaning to the word *slur* after she had a few.

❀ Lana Turner ❀

She freaked. No sooner had Lana Turner boarded than she insisted on seeing a menu. "There's no caviar. I have to have my caviar," she shrieked, sounding a lot like Zsa Zsa Gabor. It didn't seem to matter that she was on a morning flight, and caviar was served only in the evening. Somehow, the grand lady of exaggeration managed to endure.

❀ Jean-Claude Van Damme ❀

1. One gorgeous and sexy man. Very short, but proof positive that good things come in small packages. Unfortunately, he's married and she's by his side in the stateroom.

2. Oops, he's divorced now. But damn, he has his girl-friend with him. Bad timing.

3. Van Damme is back, but now he's married again.

4. Yes, there's hope. He's on again, and divorced again. But wait. Is that *another* girlfriend? It is. Shit.

5. He's back. He's married. That little dick is too damn busy. Spiked his food out of spite.

❀ Burt Young ❀

There are nervous flyers and then there are white knuckles. Burt Young (*Rocky*) fell into the latter category and compensated for his fear with booze. The more he drank in flight, the bigger he tipped—and the more he took liberties with his lips. Many times he would corner me in the stateroom and start trying to kiss me, and I was hardly the only one.

But Burt was all show and no go. After we arrived in New York, he would call my hotel and make plans to get together. All the while, I knew I could count on him to be a no-show. That he remembered the flight and to call was amazing in itself. Yet, you couldn't stay mad at this odd little man. He was endearing in spite of his drinking.

A certain Hollywood producer would probably disagree. This was a man that Burt obviously had some previous problem with. While the producer was at the bar, I watched as Burt quietly walked over, tapped the man on the shoulder, and as the man turned around, threw a hard right in his face. Then, without a word, Burt went back to his drink and his seat. Damn. Just writing about it turns me on.

MGM GRAND AIR

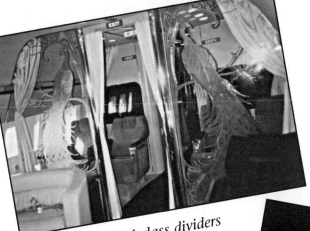

Peacock-sculptured glass dividers lead to the private staterooms.

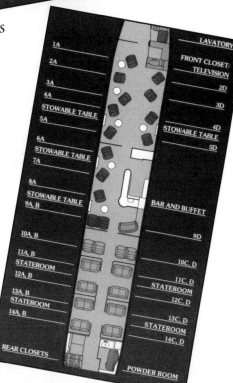

1A	LAVATORY
2A	FRONT CLOSET/ TELEVISION
3A	2D
4A	3D
STOWABLE TABLE	
5A	4D
6A	STOWABLE TABLE
STOWABLE TABLE	5D
7A	
8A	
STOWABLE TABLE	BAR AND BUFFET
9A, B	
10A, B	9D
11A, B STATEROOM	10C, D
12A, B	11C, D STATEROOM
13A, B STATEROOM	12C, D
14A, B	13C, D STATEROOM
	14C, D
REAR CLOSETS	
	POWDER ROOM

MGM Grand Air
B727 floor plan.

The bar/lounge aboard MGM Grand Air.

The infamous aft lavatory where so many joined the Mile High Club.

Diana with Freddie Jackson.

Pattee with Phil Collins on tour.

Diana with Magic Johnson.

Diana with L.A. Lakers Vlade Divac and A.C. Green.

Pat Riley, then-coach of the L.A. Lakers.

Diana with James Worthy of the L.A. Lakers.

Duff (left) and Slash of Guns N' Roses.

Pattee and fellow stew with L.A. Kings owner Bruce McNall.

Diana and the crew members with the Princess of Thailand.

Diana and Red Buttons—such a flirt and so cuddly, too.

Anthony Quinn (left) and Vic Damone celebrating MGM Grand Air's first anniversary.

Pattee and Burt Young.

5 THE COMICS

On television, the big screen, and in clubs, they all seem so funny. These men and women of comedy are filled with quick one-liners, infectious smiles, and hearty laughs, and they always seem to be happy. Put these comic geniuses on a plane and launch it to 32,000 feet, however, and something happens. The smiles turn to frowns, the one-liners are now all directed at me, and that quick wit has developed into a decidedly nasty tone, one laced with threats and other meaningless chatter. Read on.

❀ Roseanne ❀

Roseanne boarded the aircraft and dragged her enormous carryon behind her. The gay flight attendant standing at the door asked, "Hey, Roseanne, would you like me to carry that bag for you?"

Miss Two-Tons-of-Fun seized the opportunity to

turn the question into a put-down. "If you were any kind of man, you would." The flight attendant smiled and walked away.

Several years before, Roseanne and then-husband Tom Arnold were occupying a stateroom on a flight on which Eric was the purser. With only eighteen passengers, it was to be an easy workload, or so Eric thought. He had no sooner secured the plane for takeoff when he received a call for the flight attendant in the aft cabin. There was a major disturbance in Roseanne's stateroom. Hustling to the back of the plane, he was shocked to see Roseanne's daughter (the one she had given up for adoption but later reclaimed) in a knock-down, drag-out fight with her mom.

"What the hell are you doing?" he asked, summoning his butchest voice for the moment. The only response from the dueling heavyweights was more biting and screaming into the aisle. Eric was left with little option but to notify the cockpit that there was a fistfight in the rear of the plane. Given the fact that we were on an active runway, any interruption into the cockpit at that moment was considered an emergency.

The pilot brought the plane to a screeching halt, with the reply that the Arnolds—mother and daughter—had better be strapped down in their seats immediately, or the plane would return to the gate pronto. Returning to ground zero, Eric bravely threw himself in the middle of the battle of the blubbery ones and attempted to break up the fight. He eventually succeeded, but not before he endured a few bruises of his own.

The plane managed to take off, and Roseanne even apologized after a fashion. Apparently, her daughter was determined to smoke on board, and Roseanne was equally determined to see that it didn't happen. The tussle that nearly grounded the entire flight was over a cigarette.

❀ Milton Berle ❀

Uncle Miltie couldn't help himself. Surrounded by our gay flight attendants, he demonstrated the art of applying and removing lipstick within several seconds (as he had once done for his live television show).

❀ Carol Burnett ❀

First she gave us the Tarzan yell. Then we became fast friends. It was a natural connection since we both had daughters who had spent time at the same care unit. A neat, nice lady.

❀ George Burns ❀

Who could not adore and love this man? I remember a precious story about his flight on the plush 727. The lav was mirrored everywhere you could possibly imagine, including the inside of the door. Mr. Burns went into the lav and unfortunately either he forgot to lock the door or turbulence jarred it open. Thanks to the mirrors, there for all the passengers to see was the legendary George Burns on the shitter with his pants down around his ankles. It didn't faze him in the least. How wonderful to see God on his throne.

❀ Johnny and Alex Carson ❀

Johnny Carson and his wife, Alex, were on a flight that Alex obviously did not enjoy. One of the flight attendants spilled red wine on her. On the return flight, the Carsons ended up with the same flight attendant and . . . you guessed it. The girl spilled wine on Alex Carson again. Alex Carson came unglued. She couldn't contain her anger and threatened to have the girl fired. Johnny just sat back and quietly took it all in and let the wifey run off at the mouth. Watch out what you pick up on the beach.

❀ Rodney Dangerfield ❀

This comic owns one black suit and one sweat suit— probably so he won't misplace that first dollar he ever made. His nickname with the crews and passengers was Mr. Indecent Exposure, and for a very good reason. On one flight, he had fallen asleep wearing his standard sweat suit. With his big, white, flabby stomach exposed, it soon became apparent that he hadn't invested in underwear. Something white slithered out. The meal service was over, the passengers had just finished eating, and there was Rodney Dangerfield's penis staring at them on their way to the lav. Well, perhaps they didn't *have* to look but they certainly all did. The flight attendants did a quick count of the barf bags and hurried to cover his digit with a blanket. A cocktail napkin would have done the trick.

On another flight, a couple of the flight attendants were complaining that he was bad-mouthing all the female flight attendants. He was telling his traveling companion that he could sleep with any one of them because he was a star. When word filtered down to the women, they all immediately refused to serve him, leaving me to handle the duty.

Almost immediately, he started asking me questions about myself, getting ready to make me his next target. This Italian girl played along until the point when he began to make jokes at my expense.

Rodney: "So, if I marry you and promise to take care of your kids, would you fuck around on me?"

Me: "Rodney, if you married me and promised to take care of my kids, I might—just might—let you fuck me once."

The passengers clapped and Rodney laughed.

Rodney: "How about if you let me fall in love with you, and I have to buy myself an expensive wardrobe. Then, you break my heart and I lose a lot of weight."

Me: "I have a better idea. First, you buy *me* an

expensive wardrobe, you lose a ton of weight, and then . . . I'll break your heart."

The plane was in stitches. Rodney covered his ass and made peace. After unsuccessfully trying to kiss me, he conceded some sort of defeat and invited me to a premiere that evening after we got into Los Angeles. I know what you're thinking, but you're wrong. He turned out to be a perfect gentleman. We had a great time and he didn't get laid. His limo took me home. Oh yeah, he did offer to share his drugs, but I declined. I'm sure he remembers.

But wait, there's more to Rodney than you would expect. On another flight, Rodney's male companion asked one of our flight attendants (who happened to be traveling out of uniform) if *he* would like to get together after the flight for some fun. The flight attendant said he'd pass. The old "thanks anyway" routine.

Unwilling to give up so easily, Rodney thought he would try for his friend, adding $200 to the invitation. Once again, our flight attendant declined. Still not defeated, Rodney upped the offer to $500—this time for *himself,* but not for his companion. If this was supposed to make the offer sound better, it didn't work. (Between us, I do wonder what would have happened if he had offered a thousand. Nah. Forget I brought it up.)

❀ Jan Hooks ❀

A disturbing incident happened with Jan Hooks (*Saturday Night Live, Designing Women*). She was sitting in the forward cabin with her boyfriend when a *slap* was heard throughout the plane. Her boyfriend had hit her hard on the face.

Eric rushed over and demanded to know what was going on. Eric quickly learned that they were arguing over some petty bit of business. She had scratched his face to make her point; he slapped hers to make his. They had both had too much to drink and were acting like children. My friend told them as much and threatened to tell their parents if they didn't grow up, and quick. Get a clue, folks!

❀ Sam Kinison and Richard Pryor ❀

We all loved to give the individual safety demos in the private staterooms. For me, this was definitely the most fun aspect of the job. I always tried to throw in some humor to keep the stars from tuning me out and to see if they were listening.

"Ladies and gentlemen, the flight attendant standing in the aisle wearing the knee pads and with rug burns on her chin will be in the lav giving head to anyone who can remember what she says in the next five minutes." All right, that's not what I said, but that is what I *wanted* to say. It certainly would have grabbed their attention quicker than "Ladies and gentlemen, we will now tell you how you might save your life."

Of course, there were things that the passengers didn't get to see during the safety demos. Those of us who weren't doing the demos could stand at the back of the plane and make faces and obscene gestures to break the others up and destroy their concentration. It might consist of bending over and flashing them a bare ass or the finger, or pretending to masturbate if all else failed to break their concentration. One stew was so desperate that she pulled out her boobs and started twirling them. Can you imagine what would have happened if a passenger had spotted this? I don't think there would have been any complaints for the price of his ticket. How's that for guaranteeing return revenue? I wonder if Kirk Kerkorian would have personally thanked her for her extra effort for the company. Now, there's a definite employee-of-the-month nominee! My favorite distraction would be a male flight attendant dry humping a female flight attendant. That's why we want you to pay attention to the briefings. We don't want you watching what is going on behind your backs.

Sam Kinison and Richard Pryor were definitely two of my most appreciative listeners. Sam once took me aside outside the terminal and told me I was the funniest flight attendant he had ever met and the only one to keep him laughing. He sure didn't remember all the times I worked the flights when he was stoned, drunk, and out of control. We didn't like him much then, but we sure liked the newer man and wish he could have been around a lot longer.

To see Richard Pryor weakened by disease and boarding in a wheelchair was sad. But I thought I owed him some of the laughter he had brought into my life and spent the flight keeping a smile on his face. Keep the faith, Richard.

❀ Don Rickles ❀

Don Rickles boarded a flight to New York and was looking quite glum. That was my invitation to invade. I walked over and pulled down his window shade.

Startled, he looked at me and said, "Hey, why did you do that?"

"The glare off your head was disturbing the other passengers," I muttered matter-of-factly.

Score one for the stew; zero for the fat guy. I left him smiling.

❀ Jerry Seinfeld ❀

What beautiful, big-breasted flight attendant was slipping off to meet Jerry Seinfeld in New York? Rumor has it he's a big man in many ways. A real freak for cleanliness, too. He wanted everything in its place. Well, as long as that everything included his dick in a beautiful flight attendant, who could complain? I personally would have opted for Kramer.

❀ The Smothers Brothers ❀

Who else would stage a yo-yo tournament in the lounge area of a 727?

THE MUSICIANS

They're the wild men and women of rock 'n' roll. The bad boys with long hair or skinheads, tattoos, and pierced body parts. The girls who flock to their side, the groupies, the hangers-on. They're the on-top today, in-the-obits tomorrow drugheads.

They're also the legends, those seasoned veterans who have withstood the test of time and found that their flames of stardom continue to burn bright. At times seated side by side, ten deep, these pop-rock-heavy-metal superstars were only predictable to the extent that they were totally unpredictable. From the Gloved One to the Diva, they all flew MGM Grand at one time or another, each bringing his or her life story along for the ride.

❀ Bono ❀

The lead singer of the rock group U2 took the crew out in Germany. Nothing but the best from Bono. The crew could now honestly add the red-light district to their passports. Pattee just wishes she remembered the lessons she learned, but when you're drunk and on drugs, it's hard. They *do* remember the clubs Bono took them to—with live sex acts on the stage. Wow. No, better yet, WOW!

We all remember the time he took a flight attendant into the lav and told her to take off her clothes. He was impatient. He couldn't wait. He helped her remove her panties and bra. She ripped at his clothes until they were both naked. Sex? No, wait. No sex. He's putting on *her* clothes. Another flight attendant wanna-be. Nothing but the best for our passengers. We gave them the shirts off our backs.

U2's drummer loved to take off all his clothes and then just strut through the plane for effect. Well, at least no one could confuse us for Continental or ask for "More nuts, please!"

❀ Natalie Cole ❀

Back in his salad days, poor Eric was innocent enough to make cocaine runs for his roommate. One of his regular deliveries was to Natalie Cole, long before she cleaned up her act. You can imagine her surprise when Eric ended up serving her dinner in seat 5A during a trip to New York.

After the dinner service, he got up the nerve to say hello and remind her who he was. By the puzzled expression on her face, she either had forgotten Eric or was playing dumb. After he recalled her Benedict Canyon home in detail, complete with rehearsal room lined with awards, something clicked in. She became sweet in an aloof way, perhaps just as happy to have left all the drug years behind her.

❀ Phil Collins ❀

Nothing much to say about the Phil Collins tour. Phil was a class act. His group, however, kept themselves very busy on the road with the flight attendants. Especially Honey. Phil did not like Honey that much. Do you suppose he knew his horn blower was getting his horn blown by her? He may not have been happy but at least his band was being catered to, head to toe.

❀ Roger Daltrey ❀

Now there was a sight. Roger Daltrey walking down the aisle with his pants down around his knees. While that alone would not be an unusual sight when dealing with the rock groups, this guy had acupuncture needles sticking out of his body. He was quite a sight and the flight attendants had lengthy discussions on how best to utilize all those needles. Would he mind if they skewered the appetizers onto them so he could then play flight attendant and serve the rest of the passengers? Surely this group of passengers would get off on this new and unusual presentation a lot more than on our usual formal French-serve style.

❀ Miles Davis ❀

The late jazz legend kept appearing in a recurring nightmare of mine. I was in a stateroom folding one of the beds back up. I was bent over with my ass in Miles Davis's face but felt safe since I knew he was asleep. Suddenly, the strangest guttural sound came from his mouth.

"Great ass. I thought you were going to sit on my face," he said.

I turned slowly and asked, "Why? Is your nose bigger than your dick?"

Oh yeah. Now I remember. It wasn't a nightmare after all. It really happened.

❀ Placido Domingo ❀

The girls thought I was asleep on the van ride out to the airport and felt free to gossip away from my hear-all ears. Surprise. One of our attendants began to tell a story about being picked up in L.A. by a chartered plane that flew her to San Francisco for the opera and dinner. It seemed her date had rented out an entire restaurant, just so that the two of them could have some privacy. As I was about to scream with curiosity wondering who she was talking about, she whispered his name: Placido Domingo. *Mama mia.*

⚙ Bob Dylan ⚙

Bob Dylan was on board with his manager and a pretty young girl. Dylan was stoned out of his mind. Long after the meal service was finished, a flight attendant entered Dylan's stateroom to clear the dinner plates and noticed that the singer hadn't eaten a thing.

"Do you still want to work on this, or shall I take your plate?" he asked. Without saying a word, Dylan looked up briefly and then proceeded to pass out—head first into the food. "Well, I guess you're still working on it," our professional flight attendant said, closing the curtain.

⚙ José Feliciano ⚙

Only Eric would actually ask the blind classic guitarist what movie he would like to see. To his surprise and enjoyment José responded: "I'd love to see *any* movie." Go, José.

⚙ Fleetwood Mac ⚙

Eric's first charter was with the rock group Fleetwood Mac. Since Eric was one of the few not sleeping with someone in the band, he didn't last long, but he did manage to get a few good stories to carry home from the tour. Things went sour right from the start as the band was boarding. Everyone was on except lead singer Stevie Nicks. When she finally arrived, an hour late, she stumbled out of the limousine as the driver helped her gain her balance. She didn't seem to know where she was or how to get on the aircraft under her own power.

As she was helped onto the airplane, I overheard John and Christine McVie making a bet. They wagered how long it would be between the time Stevie passed out and when she woke up for her first shot of Scotch. Eric thought it was some sort of joke and giggled, loud enough for Stevie to hear.

"I want that asshole off the plane," she screamed. Somehow, Eric managed to stay. Later, a flight attendant named Debbie, who was already sleeping with the band manager, told Eric that everyone was invited to Stevie Nicks's home outside of Phoenix for a party, and Debbie asked Eric to drive. After what had happened earlier, Eric turned her down flat and inadvertently ended his job on the charter. He got canned at the hotel in Phoenix later that night.

MGM had made the decision to allow the charter customers to select their own crew. Obviously, those who cooperated with the band managers and members, sexually and otherwise, got asked back. Those who did their jobs well, but nothing else, were never seen again.

❀ The Grateful Dead ❀

Oh, surprise, doing hash in the back of the plane. So where was the Drug Enforcement Agency when we needed them? Oh yeah, I forgot, they always look for the big busts. It was little wonder that the senior flight attendants never got to work these rock charters. They never would have tolerated the kind of stuff that went down. At least Jerry Garcia tried to restrict the smoking section to the staterooms, since otherwise the flight crews would have ended up getting contact highs and becoming useless. And no pot when kids were on board. Thanks, Jerry. We miss you.

❀ Guns N' Roses ❀

At their concerts, there were hired hands who went out into the audience and selected between forty and fifty young, pretty, and sexy girls. The bimbos (as they are referred to by the group) are given backstage passes and escorted to a holding room (like cattle). The rock stars then secretly viewed the bimbos from another room, picking a few who would be invited to party, or, well, you know. The unchosen had the privilege of waiting . . . and waiting . . . and waiting. Wake up, little girls. On occasion, even flight attendants were asked to go out into the crowd to make the bimbo selection. Sisterhood?

Another time Slash, who was never without a fifth in one hand and hash in the other, disappeared without a trace. Finally we found him out on the wing of the plane, naked. (Yes, we were on the ground.) It seemed he had arranged for his photographer to take some pictures of him in the raw. Christmas cards, perhaps?

Soon after the Guns N' Roses charter, which took us to Japan, Australia, and New Zealand with the group, two flight attendants who had worked the tour were on a scheduled flight from L.A. to New York. They recognized lead singer Axl Rose's fiancée, Stephanie Seymour, as she was boarding the plane with someone *other* than Axl. There was nothing unusual about this except that they had booked the stateroom, hurried through dinner, turned out the lights, and pulled the curtains. Another entry into the Mile High Club.

When Stephanie emerged, she suddenly realized why the flight attendants looked so familiar and begged them not to say a word—especially to Axl. They, of course, had no intention of being the messenger of this news. They knew full well that if they did anything to piss Axl off, they were off the tour in a flash, sent back to L.A., never to cross his threshold again. Dumb, they weren't.

Here's a little odd sight. Apparently, Duff had a routine remedy to keep from throwing up just before takeoff. Go ahead, try this the next time you are flying. Press your head into the seat and stand on your head. What I do find really odd is that no one seems to think it's strange.

The flight crew would often party with Guns N' Roses. One time they were picked up by Rolls-Royce limos and taken to a club that had been reserved for the private party. Champagne flowed and lines of coke were provided for all, including the crew. Duff and a blond flight attendant went into the men's room for coke . . . and sex. Into a stall they went and it was wham, bam, thank you ma'am! The one little item that didn't get utilized was a rubber. Oh, the heat of the moment. Oh, the effects of booze and coke. Hello, doesn't anyone remember the word *AIDS*?

Of all the rock groups, Guns N' Roses was the most homophobic. Poor Eric heard about their attitude toward gays all during their tour. Big mouths, small minds.

❀ Michael Jackson ❀

While the world was looking for Michael Jackson, there he was with Elizabeth Taylor aboard an MGM Grand charter. In a stateroom wearing a surgical mask and with blankets covering him, Michael was too spaced out and weak to function. He was such a mess he couldn't even feed himself. Elizabeth did it for him, sweet baby.

Later, he slipped out of bed and either couldn't or wouldn't help himself up, preferring to whine like a baby for help. Once again, it was La Taylor to the rescue, lifting him up and returning him to bed. On the window's edge sat a framed picture of a young boy. At one point, the flight attendant did a quick check of the stateroom and saw movement under his blanket. Was that turbulence? She didn't want to stare . . . or know.

❁ Andrew Lloyd Webber ❁

Not a singer, but he's put a lot of music in their mouths. At the height of *Phantom of the Opera,* Andrew was a little too shy to hit it off with our flight attendants. Perhaps it was his approach.

He sent his manager over to a flight attendant who was deadheading and traveling out of uniform. "Mr. Lloyd Webber thinks you are very beautiful and would like to know if you would join him for dinner after the flight."

"No, thank you," she responded.

When the word was carried back to Andrew, he thought that perhaps a personal invite might do the trick. Taking her hand in his, he held it to his lips and stroked her face ever so gently, saying, "I think you are so beautiful. Please join me for dinner."

The answer this time was the same. "Thank you, but no." Silly girl. As for me, I was jumping up and down trying to get his attention, but he never seemed to notice.

On another flight, Andrew turned down the first course of his meal—a bowl of soup. Nope, he wanted no part of it—or, at least, not until everyone else had finished their own bowls, and he started to hear rave reviews about it. He called the flight attendant and informed her that he had changed his mind. He did want soup, after all.

"Mr. Lloyd Webber," the stew replied, "I don't think there's a drop left." He demanded that she find some—and quickly. Not wanting to disappoint the famous composer, our professional flight attendant informed my Italian friend working in the galley. Quicker than you could sing "Music of the Night," dirty soup plates were pulled out of their storage bins and scraped for all remaining drops. Finally enough phantom soup was salvaged for Mr. Lloyd Webber.

❀ Patti LuPone ❀

She sang her favorite songs from *Evita* (in which she sang the title role on stage) just to pass the time. Classy lady. Classy voice.

❀ Madonna ❀

In our "Ain't Love Grand" department: Madonna and then-hubby Sean Penn were relaxing in their stateroom as Madonna rubbed Sean's feet. They seemed the perfect couple. Fast forward several months: Madonna in the aft jumpseat on the airphone screaming "Son of a bitch!" at the very same Sean and adding several more expletives after slamming the phone down. Yup. Love's grand all right.

The princess and the pea. Madonna had a special couch custom made for the plane to hold her over-exposed body and ego. It cost only $25,000. Not that money really mattered. What mattered on this particular charter flight were the rules.

Rule Number One: Only three people were allowed in the main cabin with Madonna. Rule Number Two: Only one flight attendant was allowed up front with her—"males only." Rule Number Three: She insisted that a curtain be hung behind the cockpit door because she didn't want to see the cockpit crew when they came out to use the lav. Rule Number Four: The dancers, staff, and band members were sequestered to the back section.

It was funny how all rules were off when the plane suddenly dropped hundreds of feet in a split second. The flight attendants working the back of the plane hit the ceiling and then the floor. Madonna made an appearance explaining that she was suddenly concerned about "her girls"—so concerned that she wanted another pilot.

And about "her girls"—the injured flight attendants were told by management: "You can't see a doctor while you are on the road. If you feel that bad, then come home." As usual, if the enemy doesn't get you, the friendly fire will. No purple hearts for these girls. Just bruises.

More Madonna magic: During that short span of life when the Material Girl was dating Warren Beatty, the pair showed up in the MGM Grand Lounge in New York. Among the celebs present were Veronica Hamel and Elaine Stritch. Madonna took one look, turned to Warren, and said loud enough for all to hear: "Let's not sit with those assholes." Funny, that's exactly the same word the other passengers used for her.

❀ Dolly Parton ❀

She shrank every time we saw her. We knew we would be seeing a lot of the pilots out in the aisle when Dolly was on board. She was always wonderful to everyone around her and always had a great-looking male companion with her. On one flight, Bette Davis was also a passenger and Dolly was in awe. She desperately wanted to meet her and wrote a note requesting just that. Our purser delivered the note, and Miss Davis said, "Bring her on." The two were introduced and visited. It was our pleasure to bring these two ladies together.

❀ The Artist Formerly Known as Prince ❀

Who the hell knows what to call this guy now, but when he flew with us, he was just plain Prince. But it didn't matter what we called him since he wouldn't speak to any of us anyway. We were informed by his manager that *he,* and he alone, would speak for Prince. Since Prince could sing, I can only presume he could talk, but I swear I never heard a word pass his lips.

❀ Keith Richards ❀

The guitarist for the Rolling Stones was always wasted and nearly always passed out. What an easy passenger.

Just step over him. The other band members (and even the backup band) never missed an opportunity on the ground to skinny dip with the flight attendants. A cleaner group, obviously.

❀ Diana Ross ❀

If Cher was Bitch Number One, and Farrah Fawcett was Bitch Number Two, guess which bitch Diana Ross was? None. We called her Cuntessa. Well, she was married to a count, or whatever the hell he was supposed to be. While she screamed insults and dictates to the crew, we were told in no uncertain terms not to speak to the count. We were hired help, plain and simple.

Now, before you think all this is sour grapes, let me admit that the woman looked great. After all, she had given birth to five kids and was no spring chicken. Maybe a midlife crisis or the exhausting schedule of her life accounted for her moodiness, but it certainly couldn't excuse her rudeness. Even if her name wasn't on the passenger manifest, we could usually guess she was coming aboard by the appearance of a truck pulling up next to the plane and unloading an endless amount of Louis Vuitton luggage.

After the luggage, the Diva and her entourage would sweep on like a tornado. The crew prepared for a very long flight, and we all knew we would be spending our per diem at the bar later trying to forget the flight *and* the woman. As I said, she screamed all her demands, and God help you if you made the mistake of touching one of her children. On one flight, she screamed, "Keep those flight attendants away from my kids," after one tried to play with her youngest. You were also informed by her that *she* would order the food for her husband. We never knew if it was a control thing or he was too inept to accomplish this for himself.

This was a woman who complained about anything and everything. On one flight, she even complained about the music that was playing as she deplaned! Screw what anyone else on that plane might want. If the Cuntessa wanted to charter a flight and dictate the shots, she should have.

❀ Princess Stephanie ❀

Princess Stephanie was enamored of one of our flight attendants. The senior flight attendant played middle-man and transmitted the message from royalty. The propositioned flight attendant came to me in shock. She couldn't believe that the princess had given her the number of where she would be staying in New York, asking to get together later.

She asked, "What do I do?"

"I'm not sure of the proper protocol," I admitted, "but decide if you want to bend at the waist or at the knees for her."

No, the flight attendant didn't take her up on the offer.

❀ Rod Stewart ❀

Nothing bad to say about Rod (or his lovely wife, model Rachel Hunter), especially since I'm about to comment on his hard ass. Not that I got to see it first-hand—unlike his lucky nurse, who not only got to travel first class but got to inject that hard ass with his booster shot of vitamins. She told me that you could crack an egg on his butt. Or was it chip a tooth?

We female flight attendants loved to watch him walk, and the pilots could never get enough of their own Rachel-watching. The little dear brought along her own special linens for our flights, and we poured a lot of specialty teas. It was the least we could do considering Rod would serenade us over the intercom—something Bruce Springsteen liked to do, too.

As nice as Rod was, his manager would strike fear into the hearts of most. I, however, loved the man. I remember first meeting Rod's manager on one of our flights to New York. At the time, he was a smoker, and we'd share a conversation about the wicked vice. When the FAA banned smoking, I would still let him sneak those smokes. He remembered that—and me.

I was delighted when I could work for him again on Stewart's tour. He was always kind and generous with tickets and backstage passes, which was a nice change for a flight attendant who wasn't doing a band member (or anyone else, damn it). We must have been linked cosmically or something, for he introduced me to Rod and Rachel as his ex-wife. In another life, perhaps.

✿ Vanity ✿

I have to hand it to Vanity. The pop singer never lost her cool. On one flight, the six-year-old son of a very wealthy foreign couple had an unbelievable attraction to Vanity. We were gossiping about her days with Prince (and those that followed), when she excused herself to use the bathroom. I watched as this little boy followed her down the aisle and just hung outside the lav door.

As she came out, the kid blocked the door. She went out of her way to be kind and patient with him and basically ignored the little brat. Moving past him down the aisle, she came up to me at the bar and continued to talk trash about the old days. Suddenly, she shot up two feet, her eyes wide and round. The little tyke had just shoved his little finger up Vanity.

"Whoa," I said, pulling the prepubescent creature away from her and pushing him back to his parents. When I told them what their son had done, they only laughed and commented, "He likes her."

"Well, don't you think he could settle for an autograph?" I asked, sure they didn't care.

After getting Vanity back to her seat, apologizing that all the staterooms were full so I was unable to hide her away, I gave her my MGM logo watch, which she had admired. I told her it was in honor of the new prince who had come into her life today and reminded her to always watch her back.

❀ The Who ❀

Eric traveled with the Who on their tour, striking up a friendship with their lesbian makeup artist. The pair made an odd couple, going to all the gay bars they could find in each city, while the rest of the flight attendants satisfied themselves with members of the band. Eric got the best of the deal.

7 THE PLAYERS

After years of flying with MGM, I could usually predict the future of many of the new flight attendants. And that future often seemed to revolve around the big boys of the NBA. MGM Grand had been selected as the charter carrier of the L.A. Lakers. Little did we realize that that first contract would mean the start of MGM carrying such other teams as the Chicago Bulls, the New York Knicks, the Golden State Warriors, the Boston Celtics, the Indiana Pacers, and the L.A. Clippers, and some pro baseball clubs as well. God help us. Our fresh and innocent stews were easy pickins for these physical guys.

I'll give you an example. Quite often our new hires would come from the Midwest. Usually, they weren't more than twenty-three years old, came from somewhat sheltered backgrounds, and weren't too good at hiding the awe they felt when surrounded by the fame and wealth of our famous passengers. When they discovered that they might have something these celebs found interesting, you could almost hear their brains working at the discovery of their newfound talents. Within weeks, they went from naive hayseeds to pros who "worked" the aisles like lounge singers.

I'd play Mom and give them my best shot at advice. "These people don't marry the help" and "Keep your legs closed if you want more than a one-nighter" were two of my standard lines. Typically, my advice would fall on deaf ears. Each new flight attendant thought she would be the one who was different, so it wasn't surprising when she discovered and joined the NBA in a big way. I'd watch as fresh newcomers started to plan their entire lives around these players, trainers, coaches, and announcers. The usual routine for a night out with these boys was to jump into a cab (which you paid for yourself), go up to their rooms, and jump right into an evening of screwing.

Soon, word was networked through the teams detailing who put out and with whom. These men shared women like the women shared makeup tips. Doing one player was equivalent to doing them all. If all went well, you were a hot item for a few months, then discarded like yesterday's aluminum foil. That's if things went well. It didn't always come down that way, however.

On one L.A. team, two girls were wanted by a very seasoned and high-profile player. He hit on them but neither responded. They were smart enough to have quickly learned that there was no future playing with the engaged top dog. He was not about to hurt his image for them. However, an unattached rookie with a great NBA future was a different story. That guy was the one to put your money, and your body, on. And these girls did, ignoring the top dog's demands and staying with their chosen men.

Later, however, while on the road, Mr. Top Dog spotted these girls coming out of the players' hotel rooms. The next day, he called them on it, pulling them aside and cautioning them with the line, "I can't get rid of the players, but you girls can be replaced."

Neither girl took this threat seriously. After all, he had hit on them both and everyone knew he had his share of women, on and off the road. What they seemed to have forgotten was that they were only the hired help. Hired help who seemed to be sloppy with their exit cues for, once again, he caught them sneaking out of the players' hotel rooms, in the dead of night.

Using his clout, he soon had headquarters involved. The girls were pulled off the flight and banned from any future team trips. Mr. Top Dog followed up with an apologetic phone call to one of the girls and consoled her. He invited her over to discuss how they might be able to correct the situation. His solution included having sex, which now she was only too happy to provide. Next stop: the old dump.

When the light finally went on in her brain, she was emotionally devastated, and it still wasn't over for this young gal. She left our airline and the state in hysterics after hearing the devastating AIDS news about Magic—from television, no less. When you actually look at things, who's worse—the girl or the player? A prostitute provides a service, gets paid, and that's the end of it. A young, impressionable girl looks for love, gets used and abused, then loses both her innocence and her job.

Did she deserve this treatment? Of course not. The men involved were older, wiser, and certainly out there a hell of a lot longer. Even the rookies were briefed by their team organization and other players. They were warned about the women and told what to expect. What did the airline warn these girls about? Nothing—other than to tell them not to fraternize. Obviously, the airline never heard of forbidden fruit.

We all hear about players giving back to the community by helping young children, charities, and others. Unfortunately, their charitable ways never seemed to extend to flight attendants. I never once heard about a player taking a girl aside and saying, "Let me tell you what you are doing to yourself and what to expect."

To me, the reasons were pretty obvious. First, the player might have lost a piece of ass. Second, players have no conscience. There were no consequences from their actions. They wanted something; the girls did, too.

Perhaps the airline should have realized this kind of thing would happen when we were awarded our first charter contract. The assignment was to fly the L.A. Lakers to their preseason games. When I told my kids that I would be flying with the Lakers, they were ecstatic. While they saw extra perks, I saw extra problems—only taller. As it turned out, we were both right.

The players were treated to beverages, appetizers, snacks, a wide-screen television, private meeting rooms, and our special brand of flight attending as soon as they stepped foot into our private lounge in Los Angeles. Meanwhile, I helped prepare the aircraft and waited for the players to come aboard. At five feet, four inches, I just stood there, mouth agape, as I watched the first Laker arrive. Some over seven feet tall, all bending over in half just to enter the door. I was staring at their waists, they were staring at anything they wanted to stare at. I told them all to just sit down so I could stop craning my neck.

As the players picked seats, it became a sort of pecking order that ran from superstar to star to rookie, all led by the incredible Magic Johnson. He plopped himself into seat 5A —just before the lounge and bar—and kept it. No one dared sit in Magic's seat. Then–head coach Pat Riley always sat in one of the staterooms along with Bill Berthka. Forward A.C. Green usually sat in the first seat on the right, where it was pretty quiet and he could read his Bible. It was the perfect spot for him to hear my trashy conversations with Magic. He had prayed for Johnson's redemption before. Now, he added my name to the prayer.

James Worthy, one of the finest small forwards in the world, just sat there quietly and took it all in. Chick Hearn and Stu Lantz, the Lakers' play-by-play announcers, sat in another stateroom together, keeping to themselves. Chick immediately nicknamed me the Crazy One. Gary Vitti, the young trainer, became my closest NBA friend and confidante.

As that first charter flight took off, it was checkout time. It worked both ways. We assessed everyone's personality and likes; they checked out our bodies and availability. They didn't think we noticed, of course, since we were busy running up and down that aisle. How wrong they were.

You could actually hear their minds at work. When you walked down the aisle, they checked out your ass. When you bent over, they looked up your skirt and evaluated your legs. When you were walking toward them, it was tit time. Were they too firm, did they jiggle? Does she, will she, could she, and how soon? And that all-important one—how old is she? God forbid you accidentally made eye contact during this ritual. They would be immediately convinced, "Yeah, she wants me." Well, they were usually right.

In-flight shopping was the order of the day for these guys, who basically had their pick of the flight attendants. The same flight attendants who two months earlier would have crossed the street to avoid a black man suddenly were throwing themselves at them. The fame and money coupled with the prospect of a well-endowed man was too much to resist. It was Christmas at 35,000 feet every day.

After a grand-class flight, with all you could eat and

drink, the buffet followed you to your room. These guys had it all. Come to think about it, so did we. Flight attendants were a perfect fit for these pros. I'm sure they felt a little safer with us, at the very least.

God knows that a lot of the women who made themselves available for screwing had their eyes full of dollar signs. There could be big dollars made out there. The scams were waiting. Drug the player and rob him. Threaten to sue he raped you, hit you . . . it was endless. Or really hit the jackpot and get pregnant by one. So in some ways it made sense to sleep with the players. And for the players, it made sense to pursue the flight attendants. They knew them, hung out with them, and the price was right. If someone better came along, just stand up the flight attendant. She would always be there.

I remember a story *Cosmopolitan* ran on sex and athletes. Our airline and flight attendants were mentioned. Boy, the *Cosmopolitan* reporters missed the real stories. There were so many of them, that article could have been done as a series. Here are some they missed.

❀ Patrick Ewing and Charles Oakley ❀

New York Knicks center Patrick Ewing and forward Charles Oakley uncoiled as they stood up from their seats on the plane. It was hard to believe that our Honey had both these guys. When we took the team to Barcelona for the McDonald's Open, Honey actually tried to be in two places at once. What she finally was forced to do was spend one night with Ewing and the next with Oakley. Same hotel, same floor (and not a bad floor—the top), different nights.

The fact that she was servicing what seemed like the entire New York Knicks basketball team gave me a great idea. It would be fun to track their performance on the court after a night of love with Honey. Perhaps it would even be possible to predict the outcome of a game depending on her enthusiasm that morning. Come to think of it, we might be able to get Honey or a few of the other flight attendants some big bucks from the opposing teams during playoffs. I mean, if the players they *are* sleeping with are too cheap to lavish them with gifts, why not get something from the players they aren't sleeping with?

❀ Tommy Heinsohn ❀

A star of the Boston Celtics in the late 1950s and early 1960s, Tommy Heinsohn continued to shine as half of the Celtics Hall of Fame broadcast team. They do get kinkier as they get older. This man called a certain flight attendant nonstop, whether on the road or off, and was really heavy into the phone sex.

The flight attendant managed to get all her household chores completed while he got off on the other end of the phone. She confessed she even learned how to do her nails while moaning at the appropriate times. She found the hardest part was not laughing out loud. Buff the nails, moan, buff, squeal, buff, breathe hard, buff, ahh, what a shine.

Things seemed to be going along at their kinky best, when suddenly the relationship was over, right along with the playing season. Perhaps he found that a 900 number was cheaper.

❀ Earvin "Magic" Johnson ❀

Magic and I had each other's number immediately. The man had "I love women" written all over his face. He was a player . . . as an occupation and as a pastime. He knew immediately that I wasn't. We were both flirts, enjoyed being the center of attention, and fought for the last word. We started giving each other shit from the start, and the players loved hearing every word.

He would proposition me and I'd pin his ears back. Over and over and over. It became apparent not only that Earvin had my number but that all the players discussed us. I realized this when I went out for drinks with one of the staff. When it became obvious that there would be no sex, the guy said, "Earvin said I'd end up with a stiff dick in my hand at the end of a night with you. He was right." Ah, sweet notoriety.

My most embarrassing moment in flight, next to deplaning passengers onto an active runway, occurred with the Magic Man. I was bringing him one of his carry-on bags while we were taxiing down the runway. I bent over to set it at his feet, when we hit a pothole or something. I tumbled head first into his crotch and he, gentleman that he is, grabbed my head to help me. The players saw everything that was going on and became hysterical at the sight.

So there I was, my head in his hands, between his legs. What else could I do? I said loud enough for all to hear: "Let go of my ears. I know what I'm doing."

Releasing his grip, he came back with, "Couldn't stay away from it, huh?"

"Yeah," I admitted, straightening up. "That's right. But notice how little time I was down there?"

It was common knowledge that Earvin played as hard off the court as on. The sex started before the team even left the Forum. It was plentiful and never ceased. The girls were offered up or chosen from the court. The players were solicited at the games and out the door to the buses, planes, and hotels. The women waited for them everywhere and knew their schedules and haunts. They were in the lobbies and hotel corridors. Waiting and circling like vultures.

Some of the girls with whom Earvin played let it be known, and others were more secretive. I do remember warning him about one girl who was known by all of us to be a pathological liar. He was a big boy, but I was concerned when his marriage to Cookie was imminent. (Funny, I warned him about a talker and then ended up writing this.)

Very few could resist this man's charm. Maybe it was the heart and soul that I could see and feel when

I was with him. So many of the players had neither. If they did, it was reserved for the chosen few. Maybe it was the fact that he was never too busy, too elevated, to acknowledge you. As easily as he could play with you, he could sit you down for heart-to-heart talks.

When I was at the Forum for a game, he'd wave and call me over for a hug and a couple of words. Maybe I just felt he was another of my kids. It could have been that damn wonderful smile of his. You could get lost in it. Whatever it was, I miss him. I know if we were ever in the same place again, he would still know me. When and if you bond with this man, you know it's for life.

When the news came out about his HIV status, I cried, as thousands did. I cried as I had for the friends I had already lost to AIDS and for those that I knew I would yet lose to this disease. Although we saw each other after the news and the first of his many retirements, we never really discussed it. We spoke about his children and the closest I came was asking how he was feeling. He said that he yearned for the old days, being on the road with his team. We both said how much we missed each other's company and that was the extent of our last conversations.

The one thing my oldest daughter said when I started to write this book was, "Don't write about Magic. Don't hurt him." Yet it would be unfair for me to write about others and not mention Magic—including his promiscuity. It has nothing to do with hurt. It has to do with help. If one young athlete going pro reads this and thinks twice about unsafe sex, then it will be worth it.

Unfortunately, it never works that way. Even as Magic was making his announcement, the games continued off the court for his teammates. I saw a short-lived and immediate reaction of fear from the players. But within weeks they were back to . . . fucking around. And the word from the field was that they still weren't using protection. The girls, including many of my friends, weighed the choice presented them and played sexual roulette. The game was scary then and continues to be still.

❀ Michael Jordan ❀

Big Mike. All six-foot-six of him. The all-time favorite guard of the Chicago Bulls never seemed to tire of playing with me. While Magic Johnson knew I didn't fool around, I don't think Michael Jordan ever really figured it out for sure. He called me Red and always made me sit and visit with him. Most times he would end up talking about his wife and family. He would invite me out, as he did the rest of the girls. I had been told about our flight attendants in a hot tub with Michael Jordan one evening on the road. It certainly was a plus to have those long legs and arms. A girl on each side. Which shall it be? Both? He played with them under the bubbles. They each thought they would be the chosen one. They soon found out he was playing footsie with them both. He could handle that shot, why couldn't they? Plus, he wouldn't want to hurt anyone's feelings, now would he?

When he would invite me out just to be a tease, I'd pretend to weaken and think about it. He was also the only player who, while I was working, put his hand all the way up my skirt to my ass. He was the one I didn't expect it from either. I was bent over across from his stateroom and I felt a hand slide up my leg.

As I turned around, he flashed that big grin of his and said, "You don't wear underwear. I like that."

"Do it again and you'll be writing me one hell of a check," I returned.

He apologized immediately but never lost his grin. Damn.

Month after month, we would fly together, tease each other, flirt. Often, it went beyond flirting, and he would try valiantly to get me into bed. On one such occasion, I tried the direct approach.

"Come on, Michael. Do I look like the kind of woman who would settle for jumping into a cab and running up to your hotel room to fuck you?"

Without a second hesitation, he replied, "No. Of course not. I'd have to come down to the lobby for you."

"What a witty little shit you are," I answered back, and we both laughed.

When Jordan boarded the plane, he would make a quick round and settle into his private stateroom.

Usually he remained alone, with players stopping in from time to time to have an audience with the king. Routinely, after games, the first thing to be done in flight was to pop in a tape of the game just played. The next thing, routinely, was eat, drink, and gamble. In between was flirting with the flight attendants.

For me, the hardest part about working the flights with the Bulls was Jordan. He wanted me to sit down with him and visit. Like I didn't have an entire plane to work. On any other airline, I would have been reported to the management, but on MGM Grand, what Jordan wanted, Jordan got. Even so, I felt a responsibility to the other stews and would tell him I'd come back when everyone else was taken care of.

He was one sexy man, but I simply refused to allow myself to be in the stats. He was a player that any woman found hard to resist. The charisma poured from the man nonstop. He also showed a sincerity that I found totally disarming. He seemed to really care about each of us, and even once offered me financial help. I never asked for it, of course. He had just picked up on something I had said. I was having some real hard times and was pretty disgusted with life. He asked if I was okay. Kidding around, I told him, "Nothing money wouldn't cure."

He pulled me aside and, looking concerned, asked, "Can I help you? Do you need money?"

I'd been flying for years with these men, and this was the first time one had sincerely offered to help me. I knew Jordan meant it, and I also knew that anything he gave me wouldn't be missed or even expected back. And he would not expect or demand to take it out in trade. As much as I needed the help, I never thought about it for a second. I told him how much I appreciated the offer, thanked him, kissed him, and went back to work.

❀ Bruce McNall ❀

As the owner of the L.A. Kings, Bruce McNall should have run the show. Yet McNall had only one thing on his mind while flying and it wasn't the L.A. Kings. At least if a letter I received from fellow stew Pattee is any indication.

I had Bruce McNall on my flight last week. He had a stateroom all to himself. I spent a lot of time in there. He asked me if I'd fuck him in the bathroom so he could join the Mile High Club. He must not hear the word "no" very often, because he actually seemed shocked when I used it.

The other flight attendant decided to oblige him, hoping for some money and/or Kings tickets. So off they went into the lav in the back of our DC-8. But he still asked me out when they were finished. She must not have been that great.

When we landed in New York, he asked if I'd like to have dinner. I figured he'd been taken care of so I said okay and we went to Srozzi's. He was grabbing my legs and crotch (obviously he wasn't satisfied with the on-board meal). After dinner we got into a cab and he pulled out two sets of Kings season tickets (worth big dollars) and gave them to me! I guess this was his final attempt to get me to fuck him. I grabbed the tickets and jumped out of the cab at my hotel and was off. Unbelievable. Someone else had to fuck him, yet I got the dinner and the tickets.

I did see him later at a Kings game. He was sitting with his wife. That same evening, I ran into him in the Forum Club and he wanted me to go up to his office and fuck him on his desk. Apparently this was one of his fantasies. The picture of this fat man without clothes was enough to make me run like hell for the nearest exit. You're so right Diana, "Leave 'em wanting more, not less."

These days, of course, McNall has other things on his mind. In January 1997, he was sentenced to five years, ten months in jail, and was ordered to repay $5 million for his admitted role in a scheme to scam some $236 million from banks, a securities firm, and the NHL team. Naughty Bruce.

❀ The New York Yankees ❀

Forget that you had to wipe tobacco spit off your shoes when you worked with this baseball team. The Yankees were totally out of control. On one flight, the boys decided to have a pillow and food fight, including hurling bananas. Yes, that's right. Bananas—thrown and smashed all over the plane. It was disgusting and mattered little that they paid big dollars to have the plane cleaned.

❀ The Oakland A's ❀

They were so out of control, fighting in the aft cabin, that the flight attendants resorted to standing on the seats and screaming at them to "shut the fuck up." They never got to fly our airline again.

❀ Charles Oakley ❀

The Knicks were probably the worst NBA team with whom to travel because of Charles Oakley. There seemed no boundaries to his antics and childish temperament. Unfortunately, the more valued the player, the less support you could count on from the coach. Charles Oakley was a *very* valued player. And then-coach Pat Riley definitely had his hands full with this man. Oakley had a very large ego, however, so if you kissed his ass or were young and beautiful enough, you could breeze through the flights.

My first encounter with this team was bad from the start. At the time, I had no idea that my friend Honey had slept with Oakley (or with Patrick Ewing, for that matter). I was not aware of the hidden agenda between these three people. I had heard that the team was a difficult one, but I had always won my passengers over and wasn't worried.

Patrick Ewing asked if I was new since he didn't remember seeing me. I mentioned that I usually stayed with the L.A. teams, but my friend Honey wanted me to work with her for the month. I added that the Knicks had a reputation, to which he responded, "So do you girls." Touché. And look out.

After Honey had slept with the buddies Oakley/ Ewing, they treated her really shitty on the flights. Now, unknowingly, I would be included in their little vendetta. The flights with them went from bad to worse. Honey, the little instigator, sent me to Oakley with everything. She knew all too well that it would be only a matter of time before he did something to piss me off and I would handle him royally. I didn't disappoint her and neither did Charles.

I give him what he referred to as "'tude." Honey, never at a loss for words, mentioned to him that he ain't even *begun* to see attitude. The challenge was drawn, and I knew it. At the end of that first flight, we were standing as usual by the aft door and stairs, waiting for the team to deplane. We handed each player his coat and carryons, uneventfully. And then came Oakley's turn to leave.

He looked down at me and gruffly said, "Carry my bags off for me." I looked at Honey, who was now snickering because she knew what was coming.

"I'm sorry," I said. "What was that?"

He got closer to my face and said, "Carry my bags off the plane for me. My back hurts."

The Sicilian in me now took control of my mouth. I looked up at this child in a giant's body and said, "Carry your own fucking bags off, and if you can't, I'll be glad to kick them off for you."

I don't think he could have been that surprised at my response, but he obviously didn't know how to react and the other players behind him were listening. That did not set too well with Mr. Ego. "You got an attitude," was as good as his comeback got. Well, it never got any better between us after that. He would punish me by throwing food all over the plane and pounding the call button. This really pissed off the cockpit crew because he didn't have the common sense to stop during takeoff or landing. The cockpit would want to know what the emergency was. I'd explain and then have to make the child stop.

Even Coach Riley would get pissed but had very little control over this bad boy. Finally, I spoke to the trainers since we were so tight anyway. I asked if Oakley had to play in the next twenty-four hours. They panicked at that question. "What are you going to do to him?" they wondered out loud. "Not spike his food!"

Okay, I admit it. Our reputation had preceded us. It was easy to add a little something to a meal without anyone ever really being the wiser until it was too late. We had done it before, and these guys knew it. There was always the Visine trick. That would have the victim spending hours in the john. I've seen the galley flight attendants take a piece of meat and clean the floor with it and then serve it. Girls had pulled out their pubic hairs and slipped them into someone's food. Spitting into drinks was so common, even I became afraid to drink anything another flight attendant touched.

On one occasion, another girl was really pissed off at a passenger and said she'd had enough. Mumbling to herself, "White wine, I'll give him wine," she took a wineglass into the lav, peed into the glass, then topped it off with a floater of wine and proudly delivered it to the passenger with her best flight attendant smile.

As amazing as this no doubt seems, it was not the ultimate. That masterpiece belonged to another flight attendant who actually took a piece of meat into the lav and rubbed it around the inside of the toilet bowl . . . then served it up. How no one ended up hospitalized, I have no idea.

"Not spike the food," the trainers asked again. I never answered. They got up and immediately went to warn Oakley. That man went without food or drink from that point on. The crew got such a kick out of it, and I must admit even I was slightly charged over the power trip. Here, all the other players had our wonderful meals and limitless booze and beverages—except for Oakley, who was pretending that he wasn't hungry. I loved it. I knew I didn't have to do a thing to his food because he wouldn't touch a thing. He had been warned that I was bent on revenge. And I was.

Knowing I was not going to bid their flights anymore that season, I decided on action. The weather in New York was especially brutal that evening, and the players had their usual array of very, very expensive custom-made, full-length leather or fur coats. Honey and I dug out our Krazy glue and plunged into the aft closet. We set to work gluing every buttonhole, lapel, and pocket we could find. It gave us great pleasure to watch the freezing wind hit these men and see them try to get their hands into their pockets. We raised those aft stairs and closed the door as soon as we could. Don't let the wind hit you in the ass, boys. We laughed all the way back to L.A. Happy Trails to You, Bye Bye Knicks! Now that was "'tude," Charles. That was "'tude."

❀ Sam Perkins ❀

This six-foot, nine-inch player really liked to play with one flight attendant's head while on the road. He would make a date with her, and she would trade trips, pay for a hotel room, and dress in sexy lingerie only to get stood up. The star Lakers center used her up until something sweeter came along. She subsequently became quite attached to the L.A. Clippers, and had a major thing going with that team's trainer.

❀ Scottie Pippen ❀

The six-foot, seven-inch forward for the Chicago Bulls stayed in his own stateroom and hung out with Horace Grant a lot. They even swapped girls. Six-foot, ten-inch Horace got Scottie's throwaways.

❀ Pat Riley ❀

"Yeah, I've been happily married for years, but you still gotta have other things going on. You'll find out when you get married." Advice from the master motivator or plain old rationalization? This must not have been the best sales pitch for seducing an engaged flight attendant because it sure didn't work. As many as five phone calls a day, offers of tickets to the games, lunch, dinner at the Rainbow Room; it didn't work. The stunning young girl wanted no part of this married man.

If nothing else, Pat had taste and wanted only the best of the girls. Since all the flight attendants I knew found him to be really hot, I'm sure he scored. (Although I know for a fact that he lost out to Lakers guard Byron Scott for another flight attendant's affection and attention, too.)

❀ Bill Walton ❀

Onetime star turned NBC announcer Bill Walton was still a player. He met a stew for drinks after a flight. It seemed he had heard her say "I'm having an acid flash-back" when she forgot to deliver a drink to Clipper announcer Ralph Lawler. The Dead Head's ears perked up at that comment and suddenly he asked the girl out for a date. Another flight attendant had come with her to the bar, but she split right before dinner.

Walton had the cab drive them all over town trying to find a nice enough restaurant. Or so he said. In reality, he was attempting to locate a place that was good enough for him, but where he wouldn't run into the coaches, players, or other announcers. They were constantly interrupted by autograph seekers, but he was always patient and accommodating with fans.

A really nice guy, he talked about his speech impediment that he struggled so hard to overcome, his sons, and his poor mangled body from years of playing. After dinner, he took her back to her hotel. At their next stopover, he asked her out again.

This time, he picked her up for lunch and a movie. Later, he invited himself up to her hotel room to talk. But, oddly enough, once he was up there he didn't seem to want to talk after all. He wanted to romp. How do you keep a seven-foot-tall man off you when he wants on? Use your head? No, use your mouth. It seemed the woman he was dating didn't give great head, and our flight attendant was an expert.

In any case, a month went by without so much as a phone call. Then she heard the news that he had gotten engaged. No matter, since on their next flight he followed her around the plane asking to get together again. He wanted more. Not interested in casual sex, and not particularly interested in him, she turned him down. Still he kept trying. Finally she looked up at him and a little too loudly said, "Do I look like a fucking Seven-Eleven to you?"

Oh, the shock on his face. He gave it a rest for the moment but decided to give it one last shot as he left the plane. Again, she told him no and thought it was settled. Later that night, he continued to call her room, begging to meet up with her. The word *no* seemed to be missing from his vocabulary.

8 THE GAMBLING

If you think that Las Vegas and Atlantic City have a choke hold on gambling in America, you never flew the really friendly skies of MGM Grand. Many of our charter flights turned into major money-gaming sessions that involved some serious play. The NBA teams were the most indulgent by far.

As soon as we could set the tables up in flight, the cards came out and the gambling began. The thousands of dollars on the tables were a sight to behold. The Chicago Bulls alone kept a couple of staterooms busy with this pastime. Michael Jordan and Scottie Pippen very seldom sat or played together. They seemed to keep their distance from each other on the road and off the court. Jordan gambled with his group and Scottie with his.

The players would gamble on everything. I learned that the first time I flew with the Warriors. Chris Mullen asked me to kick off my heels. The guys had a bet on whether my toenails and fingernails were polished the same. Boys will be boys.

The Clippers were just as bad. Once they started tossing those hundreds around, their minds wouldn't allow anything to interrupt their concentration. The players would barely look up from their game to shout out for more drinks, for more this or more that. I learned how serious the gambling was on one Clipper flight. I was running amok trying to keep up with their demands and one of the players had stretched his two-mile-long legs out into the aisle. Of course, I discovered that fact too late and went flying over his legs, doing a half-gainer twist into an Olympic fall.

When the cabin lights were down low, we would try to throw a white napkin on their feet just so we wouldn't hurt ourselves. Well, that evening we forgot. Down I went. When something like this happened it was usually more embarrassing than painful. With these guys, hurt or embarrassed—it was all the same. Without looking up from his cards, Ron Harper said, "Dirty Diana is on the floor." If anyone else cared, it sure didn't show. As for the player whose legs had caused my fall: He was busy checking his million-dollar limbs.

I pulled myself up off the floor, saying, "No, please don't concern yourself. I'm not hurt. I'm fine." I love talking to the air. I suppose if I had really wanted their attention, I should have said, "Boys, I'm down here on the floor because I'm horny as shit." *Now* I think of it!

The gambling wasn't strictly an NBA obsession. The

baseball teams were even more eager to toss down their money and far ruder about doing it. These men couldn't or wouldn't wait until we were off the ground. They fought with us, wanting to have the tables up before takeoff and to stay up during landing. They didn't care that they were putting their lives—and ours—at risk in the event of an emergency.

On one flight, a senior flight attendant tried everything to get the table down for landing and finally scooped up the tablecloth with cards and money and walked off with it. They went crazy with screams and threats and tried to get her fired but settled for having her banned from future flights with them. Athletes weren't above grabbing, shoving, and pushing around any of the flight attendants, male or female, to get their way. They didn't hold back if they wanted something. Baseball players in particular were the most nasty.

On any other airline, these men would not have been able to get away with this kind of treatment or with such threats against a crew member. At the most, they would occasionally have their hands slapped by management. MGM would push the issue only if an anonymous call went to the FAA regarding the tables being down for takeoff or landing or if a flight attendant threatened legal action against a player. Then management stepped in and threatened the team.

I'm not sure whether some baseball players were born pigs. I do know that they behaved like pigs from the moment their money hit the tables. In addition to their endless demands for food and drink, we couldn't get through five minutes without their chewing tobacco landing on some part of us. At first, most just spat wherever and whenever they wanted. Finally, we resorted to passing out paper cups for them. What a joy to pick up at the end of each flight!

Once the tables went up, we would literally have to pry the fingers of these men off their cards and money to get them to stop playing. Even when we managed to stow the tables away, they didn't stop, moving instead to the aircraft floor. We would then have to step over the players and their stacks of money.

God forbid that you stepped on anything. I remember telling my gynecologist when we first discussed my impending hysterectomy that I wanted a Dustbuster installed in place of what was about to be removed. The money that I could suck up between my legs not only would pay off all my bills but also would be a great retirement package.

The only time I saw higher stakes was on Japanese charters. At least the Japanese tipped the crews. We could make up to $1,500 each, but we worked for every penny. Their hands would reach for every possible body part. I was hoping that being a brunette would relieve me from some of the attention, but I guess once they were partying they didn't give a damn. They grabbed your ass, slid a hand up your skirt, or pulled you onto their laps for a little kiss.

There was only one thing that was worse—their damn cameras. It's bad enough being pulled off your feet into someone's lap without having the move documented by Eastman-Kodak. Despite the fact that they had their hands all over you, they always seemed to find an extra arm to point one of those tiny 35-mm jobs in your face and flash off a bulb brighter than a klieg light at Mann's Chinese Theater. The real gamble, of course, had nothing to do with cards. It was far more a game of chance that one of those shots would end up in the hands of their very innocent and proper wives back home. *Sayonara,* boys.

9 THE BOSSES

Around the office, the palace, the neighborhood, the studio, these guys and gals are in charge. Big shots, big money, big attitudes. But once aboard MGM Grand, they became specimens to be watched with humor and amazement. There is very little in life that I find surprising, but even I have to admit that the behavior of some of the bosses who boarded our flight deck was one for the book. This book.

❀ Francis Ford Coppola ❀

He boarded the flight and carried on a conversation with a sexy, blond motorcycle-riding flight attendant. He invited her out to dinner later that night after they arrived in New York. He picked her up by limousine at her hotel and took her to Little Italy for dinner.

Now the scary part. He said he was not really the great Coppola. He was merely his look-alike cousin impersonating the real Coppola. The real Coppola was in an institution right then. Yet, Coppola or not, was she interested in getting together again? She went along with the ruse. They met and dated a few times, only now he confessed he was the real Coppola, after all.

She had to listen quickly, for on date number three, he wasn't Coppola anymore. Coppola or not, he had a little request. He asked if she would dress up in some sexy lingerie and have a catfight with another woman. He liked to watch.

Flight attendants can smell power, wealth, and fame in a hurricane. She knew all along, of course, that this was the *real* thing, but despite the fact that she rode a motorcycle and liked leather, she wasn't interested in kinky stuff and told him so. In particular, she wasn't interested in someone who couldn't make up his mind about his identity.

"I'll pass," she told him.

Regardless, he kept calling and left many messages. I'm curious. If she had returned his calls, who would she have asked for? Bye, Francis.

❀ Larry Flynt ❀

Larry Flynt, owner of *Hustler* magazine, is a large and wheelchair-bound man. On an evening flight into New York, everything that could go wrong did. His flight finally arrived into JFK in the wee hours of the morning. The only ground personnel left to assist Mr. Flynt was a small, ninety-pound man.

The senior flight attendant did her best to assist, but she was rather petite as well. As these two light-weights were trying to get Flynt into his wheelchair and off the plane, they struggled with his sheer bulk. They misjudged his weight, missed the wheelchair, and dropped him to the floor.

As he hit the flight deck, so did his very full colostomy bag. It fell on the lovely flight attendant's feet and exploded. Being a seasoned professional, she handled it well. She loudly started dry heaving at the sight and smell covering her feet and shoes, proving beyond a doubt just how shitty our job could be.

❀ Gary DaVid Goldberg ❀

The creator of TV's *Family Ties* and *Brooklyn Bridge* was a real family man, traveling often with his wife and children. On one flight, he had observed Robert Klein and me spending quite a bit of time talking. At the time, Klein was going through a divorce and we commiserated about our marital problems. Afterward, Klein coaxed everyone into singing old songs at the bar. Gary, trying to play matchmaker, slipped me Klein's number, but I never had the nerve to call.

❀ The ReV. JeSSe JackSon ❀

He was lovely to look at and lovely to listen to, but forget to give him his due respect and be prepared for thunder, lightning, and hell to pay. Jackson boarded our flight with three other people and was escorted to a private stateroom. The flight attendant was frantically attempting to hang up everyone's coats and stow their carryons.

As she entered Jackson's stateroom, he was the farthest from her, next to the window. Everyone in his group was holding out their jackets, coats, and carryons for her to take. Since her third arm hadn't grown in quite yet, she took what she could and returned for more.

Jackson threw his coat at her and in a voice that could cut through rock bellowed, "You take *mine* first, before anyone else's." As his coat hit her face, her humiliation and shock were apparent. Unwilling to accept such treatment, she allowed his jacket to fall to the floor. Scary to think that I wanted this man to be president. What you see ain't always what you get.

❀ Mr. Jones ❀

Just call him the Love Float. He was the president of a major television network, and Jones was not his real name. An attractive, charming, and sexy fifty-year-old, he became friendly with two of the flight attendants on a flight into New York. He told the girls how he was moving to New York and left that evening with their addresses and phone numbers. In the mail soon after, the girls received packages loaded with gifts sporting the network logo. As expected, the girls sent thank-you notes and made plans to have dinner with him on their next trip to town.

When the appointed time arrived, the three of them went to eat at a popular nightclub. As the evening progressed, one girl saw something or someone she wanted at the bar and left the other two alone. Wasting no time, these two drank bottles of expensive champagne, danced, necked, and groped to the point where they had to move to a table behind a large palm.

After a few hours, they realized that the other flight attendant was missing and went in search of the third wheel. They never found the girl, but they did locate her shoes with the bouncer. Apparently she had had too much to drink and was put shoeless into a cab. Relieved of their responsibility, they were only too anxious to get to the hotel and finish what they had started.

As it turned out, the evening was the first of many liaisons between the flight attendant and Mr. Jones. The affair went on for months and grew into something quite torrid, by all accounts. Then one day, the flight attendant was working a flight to New York when a name on the passenger manifest caught her attention. It turned out to be the wife of the exec, and the woman was seated in her section. Mrs. Jones was charming but a bit of a lush, and spoke about joining her husband and settling into her new home. Later, the wife cornered the flight attendant in the back of the plane.

Mrs. Jones became very friendly and suggested that they meet in the city and spend some time together. At this point, the flight attendant was alternating between deciding whether she was being hit on or set up. Later, instead of calling Mrs. Jones, she called Mr. Jones. He said he was going to be really busy for a while (no kidding!) and promised to call when in L.A. She told Mr. Jones about the encounter and extreme friendliness of his wife, and all he did was laugh. Well, that was enough to make that girl walk away. "Too kinky and weird for me," she said.

Unfortunately, this experience didn't teach her anything except to make her more tolerant for the next affair. This time, she became involved with a married vice president of Warner Bros. And this time, she ended up with husband and wife together on a flight and had to cater to them both. When asked why she would put herself in this position, she responded that a man with success and power is like a drug—an aphrodisiac to her. She said it made her feel powerful and in control when she could look down and see his head between her legs. She must have been serious, because as she spoke, she had a wonderful smile on her face.

❧ John F. Kennedy, Jr. ❧

Okay. The truth is that he is as gorgeous in person as he is in his pictures, if not more so. And the poor flight attendants were so taken that they could barely function. I, of course, took care of him myself. I would have loved to have *really* taken care of him myself, but he was too busy making phone calls to some lucky woman. What's that he said? "Daryl's out of town," I think.

My own personal hero, Martin Sheen, was on the same flight, but no one left him alone long enough for me to work him, either. I slipped my card into his bag, then agonized over it. Nah, this man was so into his family, religion, and who knew what else that he would never call. Chickenshit that I am, I sneaked the card back out and settled for fantasizing.

❀ Anne and Arnold Kopelson ❀

Arnold Kopelson, the producer of *Eraser, Platoon, Seven,* and so many other hit films, would fly MGM with his wife, Anne. They were down to earth and went out of their way to be courteous and fun to have on board. They had class.

❀ Sherry Lansing ❀

She was one of the most powerful women in Hollywood, and studio head Sherry Lansing never let any of us forget it. She was demanding, rude, and constantly in our way. Somehow, she never learned the words "please" or "thank you." Just seeing her name on a manifest would get me cranky. It was rumored that one of the girls trashed her luggage as payback. Need new Samsonite, Sherry?

❀ Swifty Lazar ❀

Two lovely flight attendants told the story of being wined and dined by the late, legendary agent upon their arrival in New York. Later, they were invited up to his penthouse for a nightcap. Or so they thought. Who could blame them for thinking it would be an innocent evening? After all, he was older than God, wasn't he? But then, if George Burns could still get it up, why couldn't Lazar? Apparently, he felt he could not only still get it up, but get it up for both of them! Go, Swifty.

❀ The Mafia ❀

This group of passengers was not our usual star-studded clientele, to be sure. I was surprised to see that the Mafia had discovered our airline, but discovered it they had. As they boarded the aircraft in L.A., the flight attendants decided that an Italian should handle them and I was nominated.

I picked out the man I felt was the most respected and introduced myself in Italian. I felt like an extra working on a *Godfather* sequel. He was delighted to have a New York Italian taking care of him, and I played it up, doting and fetching, Italian style.

His entourage included a couple of gorillas in suits carrying briefcases. Those boys were not so easy to work with. They were serious—deadly serious. As we were preparing to take off, one of the girls came to me and said that she couldn't get the gorillas to give up their briefcases for stowing. I went down the aisle and, looking them straight in the eye, explained that they were going to have to comply with FAA regulations. They said forget it, in so many Italian words.

Unfazed, I reached over and grabbed those briefcases as jaws dropped. "I must take them, but I promise to return them," I sputtered in Italian, meaning business. My Italian friend working the galley saw what I was doing and could not believe his eyes.

He called me over and said, "Girl, are you crazy? Quick, give those bags back to them and beg for mercy." I laughed and went about my business. The flight continued without any further problems and I was still alive when we got to New York.

While we were waiting for our bags in the airport, I saw the crew's eyes widen as they looked past me. One of the gorillas had come back into the terminal and was walking toward us. He scooped me up and carried me outside to a waiting limo. I kept telling him I thought he had me confused with someone else, how we all look alike in uniform, and that he shouldn't take his job so seriously. As we approached the limo, the window slid silently down. The elderly gentleman I had first introduced myself to handed me a card and told me in Italian, "If you ever need anything or any-one gives you any trouble, call this number." I started to mention a few names immediately, but, shit, they pulled away. Ingrates.

❀ The Princess of Thailand ❀

Royalty are the ultimate bosses, as this story proves. MGM Grand had been chartered to carry the Princess of Thailand around hither and yon. On our first leg, the crew commented they had never seen bigger lips on a woman. Our dear Imelda, the senior flight attendant on the charter, inquired about the protocol for the princess. She was informed that it was standard practice for the commoner's head to be below the princess's head at all times. At least, this was the interpretation passed on to us. It would be optional for us if we cared to do the same.

I decided I would only bend at the waist ever so slightly. This was out of respect coupled with the fact that any lower and I'd probably have a hell of a time getting back up. My dear friend and coworker Ms. Jenny, being the perfectionist that she was, became inches shorter within seconds of spotting the princess. I told her if she bent down any farther, she would be spending her layover looking for a chiropractor.

The entourage was brought on the plane first, then the children of the princess, followed by a waft of security and the princess herself. It seemed rather odd that the princess should be the last one to get on since, after all, she *was* royalty. While readying the plane for the next leg of the flight with the royal group, I mentioned to Imelda that perhaps we should board the princess first out of courtesy.

Imelda loved the idea. And so it was. Royalty first. I was so excited that my plan just might come to pass and be easier than I thought to put into action. The police-escorted caravan arrived. Our wonderful Imelda ran down those stairs and personally escorted the princess on board first. Yeah!

The children (little royalty, to me) arrived and were seated in the staterooms. Next came the entourage, who, when they saw the princess sitting, immediately fell to their knees to crawl past her. Imelda didn't see what was happening since she was still standing at the forward door of the aircraft. I was amazed at the sight in the aisle. There was a trail of people crawling down the aisle on their hands and knees. The best part came when they saw that the children were also seated. Protocol being protocol, they were practically sliding on their faces across the floor.

I coughed to get Imelda's attention and waited for her facial expression as she saw the result of the change in plans. I fell into the forward closet, my bladder control ready to go from my laughter. My mascara was running over my cheeks and down my neck. The look on Imelda's face and the sight in the aisle was more than I had hoped for. Damn, that was so good.

Imelda was such a good sport. She only called me a

few foul names and stayed mad for an hour. I decided to work my ass off to make it up to her. I may have been tired, but the smile never left my face. I think I even laughed in my sleep that night.

❀ Nancy Reagan ❀

Eric was thrilled to be working the day that Nancy Reagan and her Secret Service escorts flew from L.A. to New York. He, of course, was initially far more interested in those sexy Secret Service guys, but that's another story. As to Nancy, perhaps he just caught her on a bad day, or her psychic wasn't around to help her answer the question he asked. Whatever, when he uttered these words, "Would you care for a beverage before takeoff?" he might as well have been speaking Portuguese.

The poor woman looked confused, then puzzled, as the question was repeated three times. Finally, those sexy guys jumped in and translated: "Something to drink, Mrs. Reagan?"

"Yes, I'll have water," she said, as if no one had ever brought up the topic earlier.

Before we get completely off the subject, however, let's backtrack to those Secret Service boys. They were all dressed the same and spoke the same, but they became quite human in short order around the flight attendants of MGM Grand Air.

I loved to poke fun at them by serving them in a black raincoat, sunglasses, and a straw wrapped around my ear like an earphone. Some of our girls even had their own special Secret Service playmates in Hawaii and enjoyed them from head to toe in the sand and catamarans.

❀ The Saudi Prince ❀

On one Saudi charter, the flight attendants bowed and curtsied for a dozen Saudi royalty. His Royal Cigar-Smoking Highness requested (make that *demanded*) that he be served by female flight attendants only. He later requested that a certain flight attendant join him in his stateroom. Once she was inside the room, he placed her very common hand upon his royal scepter. Word has it that she left him holding his royal appendage and ran.

At the end of the flight, the attendants were tipped $3,400 each, with a little less cash for each of the pilots. As for the flight attendant of choice, she got nothing special for her extra effort except maybe some ribbing from the rest of the crew for suddenly becoming so prudish in the line of duty.

❀ Joel Schumacher ❀

Joel Schumacher, the director of *Batman Forever, A Time to Kill,* and other films, traveled often with us. Sometimes he didn't need a plane to fly. He was an enjoyable passenger as long as he liked you. But if he decided there was something about you that didn't quite mesh—well, you were history in his book.

One particular flight stands out in mind. The senior flight attendant was a great-looking gay man. As he bent over to get something out of a cabinet, Schumacher's hand suddenly reached out and he cupped the flight attendant's ass. "Is this tonight's dessert?" he asked.

As coincidence had it, this was the same flight attendant Rodney Dangerfield had tried to rent for an evening. Always prepared and professional, the flight attendant turned and snapped the line, "No, this dessert is too rich for you," before walking away. Now there was one flight attendant who wasn't ever going to be supplementing his income with extra work or a bit part in a Schumacher movie.

❀ The White House Press Corps ❀

Nothing exciting to say about this group. How stuffy can you get? They were a boring lot who gave us little attention. Translation: We played among ourselves during our layovers after carting these fun-lovers across the country.

❀ The Wizards of Wall Street ❀

I got a letter from Pattee, who had just returned from a charter flight to Mexico. *Olé.* "What have I gotten myself into?" she wrote.

I just picked up about twenty guys (Wall Street types) for a bachelor party in Acapulco. I watched them kiss their girlfriends and wives good-bye and get on board. We then taxied over to the International Terminal to pick up ten prostitutes who flew in from London—on the Concorde, no less. Nothing but the best for this group.

We took off and our first clue as to the kind of activity to follow was revealed when we hit a pothole while taxiing down the runway, and the overhead bin popped open. It was hysterical to see boxes of condoms hit the floor and roll down the aisle. Funny, how the rest of the world would pack that much Imodium for a trip to Mexico. What do we know?

Within an hour everyone was drunk. Dancing on the bar and tables. At first, the girls were just about naked. Then they were totally *naked. There I was trying to pour rum and cokes, with this girl's bush in my face. Is this really what I had dreamed of my whole life? How many interviews had I gone through with MGM for this?*

Things progressed as the flight went on. Sex; blow jobs; sex shows; you name it, it was happening. I guess it was worth working the trip for the four-day layover in Acapulco. On the flight home, they were still drunk—but I think they had had their fill of the prostitutes or the prostitutes had had enough. Instead, for the next five hours, they groped the flight attendants. I can think of worse jobs than fighting off gorgeous young men and getting paid for it. Maybe it was a good idea to fly for a living after all.

When we landed, we had to shut the window shades so the wives and girlfriends couldn't see the prostitutes on board. Unbelievable? I'm never getting married.

10 THE DISEASE

As we entered the 1990s, MGM Grand was hit hard by disease—from without and within. The most devastating impact would come from the effects of HIV and AIDS on our coworkers, passengers, and friends. There was Magic Johnson, of course, a major player who paid dearly for his sexual escapades. And Tony Perkins, who had died from the debilitating disease. We had lost coworkers and friends. Then came the most devastating news of all: Eric had tested positive for HIV.

Suddenly, all the laughter, the smart-aleck wit, the flirting went out of my mind as I cried for my son and dear friend. He was determined to behave as if nothing had changed between us, but we both knew that was impossible. Every cold was examined for a potential lethal punch; every sneeze was observed by the other crew members with suspicion.

Eric had worked hard and played even harder. Despite the fact that we spent much of our layover time together, I knew that after he tucked me in, he would sneak off to Greenwich Village or the gay bars and restaurants on the Upper West Side. I worried like the mother I was, even resorting to lecturing poor Eric on the dangers to be found playing in the city of sin.

Guys in their twenties think of themselves as immortal, and Eric was no different. He was a regular at a popular club in the Village and heard about the other underground clubs and bars from the regulars there. What he wanted to find was the man of his dreams; what he discovered instead was any desire, fetish, or need fulfilled. Despite his insecurities and shyness, he managed to have his share of sexual partners. And with them came the risk of AIDS. Was he careful? He said he was, but he was obviously not careful enough. He got that damn bug.

Eric had begun dating the manager of the club. And while the affair lasted only six months, word of Eric's sexual escapades began spreading throughout the airline. MGM Grand management had very little tolerance for homosexuality, and if a gay man lost weight or looked tired, the rumors began immediately. Adding to the homophobia was a gay flight attendant named Lee (not his real name) who was openly bitchy and got laid by anybody and everybody he met.

During one brief period, Eric started to party late into the evening with this tired queen, who later proved himself to be sexually compulsive. Lee frequented sex clubs on the Lower East Side and begged Eric to keep his secret. Ironically, it was Lee who first started the rumors about another gay flight attendant. Although this flight attendant knew he was HIV positive, he had kept the news to himself for fear of losing his job and insurance benefits. He didn't have much choice.

The company and its executives weren't educated enough to deal with employees who had contracted the AIDS virus. And when Lee began to spread rumors about that flight attendant, the paranoia only got worse. Regardless of his own efforts, this poor guy soon found himself working in the corporate office and eventually succumbed to complications from the disease. Shortly after his friend's death, Eric was called into a meeting with two supervisors.

Despite his request for an impartial witness, none was permitted to join him in the meeting. The following account came unedited from him and speaks directly to the attitude that ran rampant throughout the airline.

In the meeting, one supervisor said that several flight attendants had come to her and expressed their concern over the fact that my friend had died of AIDS. She also said that these same flight attendants were worried about working with me. At first, I didn't understand what she was trying to say, but she spared little time in making herself perfectly clear.

"Well, you know, you are gay and you were a friend of his, and you were in the same class and everything," she began. "The flight attendants are

afraid that they could become infected because they work with you."

I was horrified and couldn't believe that she was saying these things to me. At the time this meeting took place, I was still testing negative. I looked to the other supervisor for support but got none. I didn't know how to handle what was happening, excused myself, and left on my scheduled flight. I did my best to avoid them and anyone from management. I chose to bid a two-month charter. I thought it best to just get away for as long as possible. I knew that they would find another person to concentrate on, and hoped that when I got back, the problem would just disappear. It was not to be.

The harassment started as soon as I returned. Before and after every flight, I was served with a note that would discredit my reputation, berate my work, and criticize my abilities. One note threatened that if I didn't give 150 percent effort, disciplinary action would be taken. It was soon after that when I discovered the most devastating news I could hear. I was HIV positive.

I struggled to make it through each day, fighting depression and the uncertainty of my future. I continued to receive threatening notes and letters from my supervisor. I was now seeing a doctor twice a month as strange and unexplainable health problems were beginning to occur. Finally it got to the point where I wasn't able to concentrate on my responsibilities as a flight attendant. It was time to take some time off, get help, regroup, and gather information about my disease.

According to company policy, an employee was allowed to take up to a year off, and I chose to exercise that option. Ironically, this leave-of-absence policy was quickly revised after I took advantage of it. Yet, my break from the grind of life in the air was exactly what the doctor ordered. I found that I was able to deal with my emotional situation and health problems, and I decided that it was time to return to work.

I don't know what I expected from management. I hoped for understanding when I met with my supervisors and told them of my condition, requesting a schedule that would not be physically draining and that would allow me to keep the necessary doctor appointments. At the time, MGM was flying only charters, and flight attendants were routinely away from home for up to a month—sometimes even longer. I knew that kind of schedule wouldn't work for me.

The response I received was both terse and unsympathetic. Essentially I was told that if I came back, I would have to work as much or more than I had previously. "We will not accommodate you," the MGM Grand management said. "Take it or leave it."

In spite of their treatment, I advised them that I would return and go through recurrent training. Their response was to demote me from my previous level, status, and pay scale. I was also informed that

I would lose my seniority for the time I was gone, and that I could not work around food (for fear I would infect the passengers and other crew members).

I was shocked. Had these people no clue how AIDS was spread? I attempted to explain the route of transmission, only to be cut off and instructed to do as I was told. I was outraged by the company's attitude and expressed my concern to a company officer. I was met with the same resistance, but I still refused to allow such ignorance to exist in my workplace.

I turned next to the Gay and Lesbian Service Center in Hollywood, and was guided to an attorney who agreed to represent me in a discrimination suit. I also discovered I was not alone. Flight attendants before me had launched similar suits against the airline. In fact, my attorney tracked down five others, and I joined the effort to force MGM to see the error of their ways.

Through it all, I really only wanted to return to work. I would have been just as happy to have gone about my business, created no fuss, threatened no court action. The other suits ended in private settlements, and eventually MGM Grand came to my attorney with an offer to settle out-of-court. As was the company's usual practice, the offer came with a nondisclosure agreement, prohibiting me from discussing the settlement. I took the money and decided to get on with my life. The airline was off the hook, and learned nothing, I'm sure, from the suit.

Would I have preferred something different? Absolutely. Rather than money, I would have welcomed the opportunity to work and to feel needed, appreciated, and respected. If the company's attitude had been different, so too would have mine. If I could have returned knowing that I would not have had the stress of a hatchet waiting to drop on my neck, I would have done it in a minute. Yet, such was not the case, and like many others before me, I found that there was, indeed, life after MGM.

Eric's departure from the airline was the company's loss. Ironically, the company itself was dying from within, a victim of its own mismanagement. When the airline had switched from 727s to the less expensive DC-8s, the passengers weren't prepared for the decline in service. It was a larger plane, and one less suited to the kind of royal treatment passengers had come to expect. The airline was on a downward spiral and there would be no pulling out of the nosedive.

When MGM hired its first class of flight attendants, our leader was a wonderfully classy man by the name of General Rodgers. He looked just like an English country gentleman. He knew how to impress our elite clientele and set high standards. He didn't last very long, unfortunately. Apparently it was thought he was spending the dollars frivolously.

He was eventually replaced with a man who thought flight attendants didn't or shouldn't make more than $25,000 a year. This man actually said the words, "Frank Lorenzo is a visionary," referring to the man who nearly put Continental Airlines in the crapper. That endeared him to our hearts immediately—especially to our pilots who once worked for Continental and quit rather than work under Lorenzo's reign. Lorenzo was so hated by his own employees, it was said that he had bodyguards because of death threats. Now, suddenly, we had one of his disciples as our leader. He seemed to be considered a hero by MGM's board of directors. And why not? He started to pare and prune his way through the airline and costs went down. So did our service.

Presidents and vice presidents came and went and we all tired of revolving-door management. Rather than fight the writing on the wall, we tried to settle into a "work with what we have" existence. I never knew if the changes that our chief imposed were of his own design or those of the board. I *do* know that with each request for an increase in pay or benefits, we were reminded that we were a start-up airline. That answer worked for the first three or four years. Later the story changed to, "Things are bad."

Granted, the first months were scary ones, when we had only a handful of passengers per flight. Eventually, however, we were flying to packed planes, and that's when our demands should have been met. Instead, we got promises, all of them broken. As morale plummeted, we threatened to unionize. The response from management was characteristic: "The doors will close before we go union." Personally, I didn't believe it for a minute, but our pilots had been there before with Continental and were not ready to risk it all once again.

I actually tried to refuse a ninety-cent-an-hour increase on the grounds that I'd have to give up food stamps, and that the increase in income might push me over the poverty level. I wasn't kidding. The airline was being nickled and dimed to death by a penny-wise, pound-foolish management that was recklessly taking its flight crew for granted.

I never let a single opportunity pass without letting them know this fact—and loudly. Needless to say, I didn't get along with management very well. Eventually, our president referred to me as "that goddamned Diana." In return, I referred to his periodic informational luncheon get-togethers with the flight attendants as the "upchuck" meetings. These sessions were designed to allow us an open forum to discuss our concerns and make our demands. It was a nice touch, the luncheons. It was the old "feed 'em and then fuck 'em" routine.

Somewhere along the line, it was decided that there would be no more passes for the crew and their families. Management didn't want us sitting next to our elite passengers. We could feed them, we could fuck them, but we couldn't sit next to them. It was the first of many benefits that we saw disappear, right along with our desire to see the airline be its best.

With the crew and flight attendants no longer

beating themselves up to make a difference, it was only a matter of time before the passengers disappeared. Don't get me wrong. It's not that we didn't care anymore. We did. We just cared more about ourselves than we did about an airline that treated its employees like necessary expenses.

We were always a crazy group, and we only got wilder. And nowhere did our behavior get more risqué than in the cockpit. Our pilots worked hard, and we liked to let them know how much they were appreciated. One way we showed them was to walk into the cockpit and bare-ass those boys, or at the very least serve their coffee with our tits exposed. Okay, my tits weren't what they wanted to see, but of some others they couldn't get enough. The new and younger flight attendants bantered about filing sexual harassment charges daily. Sexual harassment was a minor threat, however, compared to what management was doing to us all.

The charter business, which was at first intermittent, now became a larger portion of our business. We added three more planes to our fleet and at the same time we added another class of service. Steerage. Okay, it wasn't exactly like booking passage on a tramp steamer, but this was MGM Grand, where everything we did was supposed to be larger than life.

The crew moaned and bitched about the new MGM Grand Class Coach, but our pleas were ignored. Management had their heads so far up their asses they were in the dark and determined to stay there. The first flight that featured Grand Class Coach on our DC-8 was a nightmare. I had wisely opted to stay home, but old Kujo was aboard with Eric.

When the plane was empty all looked great. When filled, however, it was another story. The interior of the plane looked like a thirty-car pileup. The reclining seats had built-in footrests and swiveled back and forth. Use both together and passengers were either trapped in their seats or hit others as they moved. Our classy service became comical as we tried to dodge moving velour.

We also began to experience electrical problems. We lost power unexpectedly. The ovens stopped functioning. The audio and visual died. The fax went dead. Even the cappuccino maker lost its steam. The only things hot on that plane that day were the passengers. Mrs. Frank Sinatra and Mrs. Don Rickles, aboard that inaugural two-service flight, were the most vocal. After pointing out every design flaw aboard, they threatened to personally call Kirk Kerkorian and have poor Kujo fired.

She was reduced to hand-holding and begging for mercy. The food finally got served as the captain was about to begin his descent into New York. Flight attendants scrambled to collect plates full of half-eaten and cold food. The Three Stooges could have learned something from us that day. To make matters worse, no sooner had the plates, crystal, and stemware been tossed into the cupboard than the plane hit the runway hard—too hard. The overloaded cupboard exploded and the contents were dumped all over Kujo.

Poor Kujo was covered head to toe in food. Her panty hose were shredded. And as she opened the plane door, the sounds and sight of broken china and glass greeted the passenger service rep. Kujo was in tears and had to listen to harassed passengers threaten her even as their voices disappeared into the terminal.

Our elite clientele never did get used to having coach passengers on the same plane with them. The replacement of our plush 727s with DC-8s hit our regulars as hard as it did us, and before long MGM Grand ended its scheduled service.

The charter service continued but half our employees were laid off. All of our New York employees were given their walking papers, and more than 50 percent of the Los Angeles-based flight crew as well. For those of us who remained, we would be rewarded with more hours and less pay. As crews were separated from their families for months on end, strong marriages suffered, rocky marriages crumbled, and we even began to fight among ourselves.

Even the most seasoned of the original flight attendants dropped by the wayside. Honey, poor thing, was injured on the Madonna tour, and I took one too many hits of turbulence and was out on medical leave when the announcement that MGM Grand would begin scheduled service again hit the news.

What looked like a resurrection was merely an illusion—a ploy to sell the airline to an interested buyer. The end came on January 1, 1995, with the sale of the fleet to AIA, a freight-carrier operation out of Michigan. The flight crews were invited to interview for the few positions available. The diehards chose to continue with the next carrier. But it wasn't the same. MGM was no longer Grand, or anything else but a memory.

EPILOGUE

THE REAL
FIRST CLASS

My years of flying have taught me much about a business that takes more notice of its bottom line than it does its employees, about the lack of respect many men have for women and women have for themselves, and about the price of excessive sex and gambling on the human soul. What an eye-opener.

I also learned about prejudice—against women who looked upon themselves as sex objects and men who insisted that was the only true perspective. And about gays—misunderstood, maligned, brilliant, bitchy, funny, and creative. Straight men could learn quite a bit from these guys.

Speaking of friends, Ms. Jenny the Juicer went on one of the last of the great charters with her juicer in hand before returning home to dabble in business (ad)ventures. She remarried her ex and can now be found climbing mountains, camping out in exotic lands, and probably grazing the terrain for her diet.

Mi Amico, my Italian Robert Downey, Jr., look-alike,

ended up taking one hell of a spill in a New York hotel during a layover. He probably fell off a pair of "come fuck me" pumps—who knows? After his back surgery, he retired from the aisles in the sky. He took another fall right into the lap of Mr. Right, and lives happily cooking pasta in his love nest.

Captain Ed is as secretive as ever about his comings, goings, and whereabouts. He stays in touch, cooks me a great meal every now and again, and still begs me to sit on his face. I guess old captains never die. They just hit their knees.

Captain Foot-in-the-Mouth continues to fly and add to his Indian jewelry collection. Thanks to the sexual harassment laws, he doesn't chase the flight attendants anymore. Now, he just looks sad and follows them to their rooms at a safe distance. We haven't spoken in a long time, which is just as well since it's hard to understand someone when his mouth is full anyway.

Kujo and her Vaseline continue to fly, and they've made the rounds of several more airlines in the past few years. If you happen upon a very shiny-faced, been-out-there-too-long gal, give her a little pat on the ass for all of us. Then run like hell.

Gary left MGM before the doors closed. He has a successful catering business and now sells real estate. I'm happy to report that we have stayed on good terms and keep in touch.

Ghassan . . . ah, I worry about Ghassan. He returned to his native Lebanon and his flights are no doubt over less friendly skies these days. It's been too long since I heard from him, and I pray for his safety and miss the "true gentleman" in my life.

Imelda, I just learned, is about to divorce her rich passenger-husband. Guess she wasn't a fairytale princess after all. Well, there's always next time. It's his loss.

Body Beautiful is still a knockout, both in the movies and on TV. I get to see her once a week on her TV sit-com, and she calls often to touch base with her "mom."

Pattee went on to fly with various airlines that unfortunately met the same fate as MGM Grand. She is happily married and keeps busy running her toddler to modeling and commercial auditions. Like me, she misses the aisle, the travel, and most of all, the friendships of flying.

Honey . . . what can I say about this gal? Nothing has changed except the names. Her list of lovers grows. Now it even includes her latest discovery—the elderly. Last I heard, she was seeing a mystery writer, an executive, and a stockbroker. Don't worry about this girl. She has added sales experience to her résumé and is currently an on-call corporate flight attendant. If you're a woman and happen to hear "Whee!" from a nearby flight attendant, hold on to your man. If you are a man, just hold on, period.

Eric, my son and my friend, has continued to be my faithful child with his love, support, and nonobligatory phone calls. He holds down a full-time student schedule since returning to college. He also has a Mr. Right in his life. Yes, I approve. He never thinks about returning to flying. And yes, he is feeling just fine.

And what of me, you ask? First, not wanting to fall into the category of sky hag, which can happen after so much exposure to dry cabin air and turbulence, I have formed a close relationship with a flight attendant–friendly plastic surgeon, Dr. Ronald W. Strahan in Los Angeles, and his dynamo right hand, Ida. Oh, and for those questions that were asked by passengers: Do nipples harden at 35,000 feet, and can breast implants swell or burst? First, yes, nipples can harden at 35,000 feet—if you have the right passenger on board. As for the implants, I never saw a leaking flight attendant, but I have seen a few lopsided ones. So be careful when picking that surgeon.

As to my life today, I still take it one day at a time and do my best to handle the Crisis Clinic (which is my home) and our daughters, with the love and support of my Vietnam vet, Michael. He always managed to come back from his mental trips to Nam to help raise three "personality-packed" girls who are the love of our lives—now and forever. He never chose the easier route of being AWOL. He never bailed on them or his wacky, crazy wife. However, let's hope he'll be off in Nam when this book comes out. Isn't it ironic that when I first flew it was to get away from home, have some fun, find a husband, settle down, and raise a family? Later with MGM it was to get away from home, the husband, the family, and have some fun. I have learned to be careful in what I wish for.